Field of Fire

**NEW
ISLAND**

Field of Fire

The Battle of
Ashbourne, 1916

Paul O'Brien

1916 IN FOCUS

FIELD OF FIRE
First published 2012
by New Island
2 Brookside
Dundrum Road
Dublin 14
www.newisland.ie

P/B   ISBN: 978-1-84840-156-3
ePub   ISBN: 978-1-84840-157-0
emobi   ISBN: 978-1-84840-158-7

British Library Cataloguing Data. A CIP catalogue record for this book is
available from the British Library

Typeset by Mariel Deegan
Book design by Mariel & Justin Deegan
Printed by Bell and Bain Ltd

New Island received financial assistance from
The Arts Council (An Comhairle Ealaíon), Dublin, Ireland

10 9 8 7 6 5 4 3 2 1

For Gerry Kelly
1944-2010

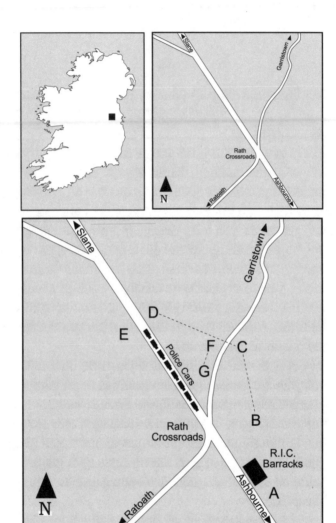

Rath Cross, Ashbourne, 28th April 1916

A. Position of Section One of Volunteers at start of fight.
B. Position of Sections Two and Three at start of fight.
C. Sections Two and Three retreat to this point after arrival of police.
D. Some of these men move to here to cut off any police retreat.
E. Belated arrival of Section Four - Volunteers exchange fire on each side by mistake.
F,G. Scene of heavy fighting along Garristown Road.

Contents

Acknowledgements

During my research for this work, I soon learned that one should not be dismayed when people warn you that they have little of interest to offer. A lot of people surprised themselves and me when they recalled family memories of that spring day in 1916. Without their stories and insights, this book would not have been written.

I wish to thank Paddy Weston and the Weston family and Lieutenant-Colonel Lawless for information they provided on their relatives. A special word of thanks to Mícheál Ó Móráin and Brigid Ashe.

For putting me on the right track, thanks are due to Brian Arnold and Fiach Ó Brin.

To Gerry Woods, cartographer, many thanks for bringing the field of battle to life.

Thanks are due to Sue Sutton, Liz Gillis and Ray Bateson who have spent many hours researching and answering questions in relation to those involved in the battle of Ashbourne.

I am most grateful to Lisa Dolan, Noelle Grothier and all the staff at the Military Archives in Dublin, Anne Marie Ryan in Kilmainham Gaol and the Irish Defence Forces staff at the Curragh Museum in County Kildare. Thanks are also due to the staff at the archives of An Garda Síochána and the Police Service of Northern Ireland.

A special word of thanks to John Galligan for ballistics advice.

As always, research for all the books I have written begins in the library. I am indebted to Nuala Canny of the Library of the Office of Public Works, the staff of the National Library Dublin, Ashbourne Library, Tralee Library and Ballymun Library.

I would particularly like to thank Mary Montaut and John McGuiggan who kindly read through the initial drafts. Both have given me wise advice and suggested changes, which I have incorporated.

I am above all grateful to: Paul Knowles, James Langton, Pauline Compton, Micheál Ó Doibhlín, Paddy Woods, Noel Davis, T. Dooley, Michael Cahill, Darren O' Brien, Tommy Galvin, Sergeant Wayne Fitzgerald and the staff at *An Cosantóir*.

I would like to thank all the staff at New Island for their continued enthusiasm in relation to the *1916 in Focus* series and in particular I owe an important debt of gratitude to Eoin Purcell.

Finally I would like to thank my parents Tommy and Rita O' Brien and my wife Marian for their continued support.

This book has been written using the available historical records both in Ireland and England. There are many people who helped with my research, and in naming some of them I can only apologise to those whom I have inadvertently left out. I would like to invite them to make me aware of any omissions or relevant information that may be included in any further updated edition.

Paul O' Brien
Dublin, September 2012
paulobrienauthor.ie

Foreword

While Dublin city acquired a certain romanticism in fictional and factual accounts of the 1916 Rising, real dramas were also taking place outside the capital city. The area where North County Dublin becomes County Meath, with its lush vegetation and green fields, saw much Volunteer activity during April of 1916.

The town of Ashbourne, historically known as Cill Dhéagláin, is located twenty kilometres north of Dublin city. It was at Ashbourne in County Meath on Friday 28 April 1916 that the Royal Irish Constabulary found themselves in action against the forces of the 5th Battalion of the Irish Volunteers.

In many of the works written on the 1916 Easter Rising, the Battle of Ashbourne has been ignored and dismissed as a side-show to what was taking place in Dublin city. On studying this engagement, however, it may be seen that the battle there was not only an integral part of the Rising, but was also a template for the future tactics and strategies employed by Republican forces during the Irish War of Independence.

The Battle of Ashbourne was a complicated and bloody affair and poses a number of questions to the student of military history. Questions arise in relation to the strategy employed by the police and the controversy that surrounded the number of casualties they suffered and if they could have been avoided. Was the action that took place an ambush, as it was characterised by the Crown, or was there much more to this battle?

With regard to the Irish side, questions arise in relation to the military competence of their force during the battle and how they managed to pull off one of the greatest victories of the 1916 Rising.

Unlike castles and cathedrals, the rural battlefields of the 1916 Rising are not easily found and require some background knowledge of the contenders' tactics, the cause of the battle and its final outcome. At first sight, Ashbourne is a piece of rural landscape, yet it was here that forces of the Royal Irish Constabulary were decimated in a bloody conflict. The object of this book is to describe the battle that took place and dispel many of the myths that have grown up around this significant engagement.

Prelude

After the implementation of the Act of Union in 1801, which abolished the Irish Parliament, Ireland was directly ruled from the Westminster Parliament in London. The rise of cultural nationalism in Ireland during the late nineteenth century reinforced the idea that the country had a strong cultural identity separate from that of Britain, which led to the belief that if the country was culturally separate then it should also be politically separate. Home Rule became the main objective of Irish nationalists, but it was not until 1912 that the Third Home Rule Bill was introduced in the House of Commons and was met with opposition by many unionists. The bill offered a limited independence to the country.

Many unionists in Ireland objected to the bill as it was seen as an attempt to force those who wanted to remain united with Britain into an Irish-controlled Parliament. In January 1913 the Ulster Volunteers were established by the unionist leaders Sir Edward Carson and James Craig to defend the union with Britain. In November of that year the Irish Volunteers were formed to defend the ideal of Home Rule. However, the bill's implementation was postponed with the outbreak of the First World War. For many nationalists the delay was unacceptable and their main aim soon became full independence from Britain.[1] The secret military council of the Irish Republican Brotherhood, which comprised Patrick Pearse, Eamonn Ceannt and Joseph Plunkett, drew up plans for an insurrection.

In Dublin city, it was the job of the Dublin Metropolitan Police and its 'G division' to uncover any political or subversive groups that were a threat to the Crown. For the rest of the country it was the job of the Royal Irish Constabulary.

The first organised police force in Ireland came through the Peace Preservation Act of 1814. The reorganisation of the act in 1836 saw the consolidation of the Irish Constabulary and the Peace Preservation Force into an Irish police force. Rewarding their loyalty to the Crown after the suppression of the Fenian Rising of 1867, Queen Victoria granted the prefix 'Royal' to their name and the Royal Irish Constabulary came into being. Distinctive in their dark green military style uniforms, they were deployed throughout the country (except for Dublin city) and were subject to military drill and discipline. The majority of constables were recruited from the same social class, religion and general background as their neighbours.

Centrally controlled from Dublin Castle, their training depot was located in the Phoenix Park. Unlike other police forces throughout the British Isles, the government believed that Ireland required an armed military force rather than civilian regulation. Its main task was the imposition of public order, but locally the Royal Irish Constabulary were considered the eyes and ears of the British government in rural Ireland, collecting information, reporting possible dissidents and applying force to impose Crown law on the local populace.[2] The force gained widespread distrust from among the poor Catholic population after the enforcement of thousands of eviction orders during the land wars of the nineteenth century. By 1901, the Royal Irish Constabulary was firmly ensconced amongst the rural Irish population with sixteen hundred barracks and eleven thousand constables throughout the country.

In the forthcoming insurrection, the Irish Volunteers would find themselves locked in a bitter struggle with the forces of the British Crown. While the Dublin Metropolitan Police would be withdrawn from the streets of the capital and replaced by units of the British Army, the countryside of Ireland would continue to be policed by the Royal Irish Constabulary. The boreens and hedgerows of North County Dublin would witness some of the bloodiest actions of the 1916 Easter Rising. What follows is the story of 1916 and the Battle of Ashbourne.

Chapter 1

Sunday 23 April 1916

On Easter Sunday 1916, orders were issued for the mobilisation of the Irish Volunteers as an independent Irish Republic was to be declared. The supreme council of the Irish Volunteers, which included Eoin MacNeill and Bulmer Hobson, was not informed of the planned uprising until the last moment. On being apprised of it, Eoin MacNeill supported the idea until he heard that the Royal Navy had intercepted the *Aud*, a ship laden with arms and ammunition. Deciding to withdraw his support for the insurrection, MacNeill issued a countermanding order cancelling the general mobilisation for that Sunday.

The military council of the Irish Volunteers accepted the inevitable setbacks that had occurred and immediately set about reorganising their timetable for the Rising.

Despite the cancellation, on Easter Sunday 23 April 1916 at 12.00 hours, members of the 5th Battalion (Fingal) of the Irish

4

Volunteers mobilised with full kit at Knocksedan, Swords, in North County Dublin. Many of the men who assembled had read the front-page notice from their commander MacNeill in the *Sunday Independent* that stated:

Owing to the critical position, all orders given to the Irish Volunteers for tomorrow, Easter Sunday, are hereby rescinded and no parades, marches or other movements of the Irish Volunteers will take place. Each individual will obey this order strictly in every particular.[1]

Many other Volunteers who had assembled throughout the country were ordered to 'stand down' by their officers and return home. The officers of the 5th Battalion knew of the planned Rising but no official orders had arrived from Volunteer headquarters in Dublin city.

Volunteers in the 5th Battalion had travelled from Lusk, Skerries and from St Margaret's. Each Volunteer company had an average of twenty to thirty men in its ranks. The Swords and Lusk Companies had the largest contingents with over thirty men on their rolls. Dick Coleman commanded Swords. James V. Lawless commanded St Margaret's. Edward Rooney was in charge of Lusk and Joe Thornton and Jim McGuinness commanded Skerries.[2] Like most Volunteer units of the time they were never near battalion strength. However, it was estimated that nearly every Volunteer had turned out for Sunday's parade, a total of one hundred and twenty men.

In the previous months, the battalion had undergone extensive rifle practice, drill exercise and manoeuvres.[3] They had also received tactical lectures from Eimar O'Duffy, who had attended Sandhurst Military College.[4]

The 5th Battalion staff consisted of the newly appointed Commandant Thomas Ashe, Adjutant Dr Richard Hayes and Battalion Quartermaster (B.Q.M.S.) Frank Lawless.

Ashe was thirty-one years old and stood over six feet tall. He was broad and muscular with fair, curling hair. A native of Dingle, County Kerry, he was employed as a schoolteacher in Corduff National School in Lusk, County Dublin. A fluent Irish speaker, and an accomplished musician, he was instrumental in forming the 'Black Raven' Pipers of Lusk. His impressive physical presence and his charisma made him an ideal commander. He was a popular officer with his superiors and his men.

Adjutant Dr Richard Hayes was the medical and intelligence officer of the battalion. He was thirty-eight years old and held a medical practice in North County Dublin. Formally the Commandant of the Battalion, he had relinquished his command in favour of Ashe, in order to concentrate on his medical practice.

Frank Lawless, the battalion quartermaster (B.Q.M.S.) was forty-six years old and was a farmer. He came from a strong nationalist background and many of his family were members of the Irish Volunteers, including his son Joseph.

In order to keep it in a state of readiness, Commandant Thomas Ashe marched the battalion to Saucertown where a tactical exercise was carried out. He then ordered Frank Lawless's son Joseph to make his way to Liberty Hall in Dublin with a message for Commandant James Connolly, commander of the Irish Citizen Army. The despatch stated that the 5th Battalion were in readiness and awaiting further orders. The young Volunteer was told to use his discretion if there was any attempt by the authorities to stop him from achieving his mission. Lawless checked his Webley revolver was loaded and holstered the weapon. Leaving Swords on Ashe's Hudson Motorcycle, it took him about twenty minutes to reach Dublin city. As he made his way through the city streets, he noticed an air of tension within the capital.

On arriving at Liberty Hall he found the building under guard by members of the Irish Citizen Army. The Volunteer was led upstairs and through a series of hallways and into a foyer. Here, the guard announced the arrival of the despatch rider to an orderly who entered an adjacent office. Commandant James Connolly called the Volunteer in and read Commandant Ashe's message. Commandant Connolly questioned Lawless in relation to the numbers that had turned out, their armaments and what they thought of the newspaper announcement.

Connolly was pleased with the positive response from the Volunteer and drew up new orders for the 5th Battalion. Lawless mounted his motorbike and returned to the camp in Swords, arriving later that night. The order from Commandant Connolly read:

All was off for the moment, but to hold in readiness to act at any time.[5]

After midnight Frank Lawless and Dr Richard Hayes drove to Dublin in order to gather further information on the situation. Having tried several prominent addresses they finally gained entry to a house on North Richmond Street and consulted with Michael O'Hanrahan and Tom Weafer. Confusion reigned among the ranks of the Volunteers. After a brief consultation it was decided that the best course of action would be to 'stand down' the men but notify them that they could be expected to mobilise at any moment. Lawless and Hayes returned to their camp at 02.00 hours and it was decided by all the officers present to disperse their companies. Commandant Ashe and Captain Coleman returned to Dr Hayes's residence for the night.

The words of Commandant Connolly's order reverberated in everyone's mind.

'All was off for the moment, but to hold in readiness to act at any time'.

That time would be much sooner than anyone expected.

Chapter 2

Easter Monday 24 April 1916

At 07.00 hours a loud knocking on the door of his house woke Joseph Lawless. From his bed he could hear his father answering the door and conversing with the caller. A Volunteer despatch courier had arrived from the city with an important message. He recognised the voice as that of his Aunt Mary, a member of the Cumann na mBan. The despatch read:

> Strike at one o'clock today.
> P.H. Pearse.[1]

Frank Lawless called his son and told him of the order. Taking Ashe's motorcycle, Joseph headed off to the house of Dr Hayes in order to deliver the message to Commandant Ashe.

On reading the communiqué, Commandant Ashe immediately issued orders to mobilise the four companies of the battalion.[2]

Joe Lawless headed off once again to inform Ned Rooney at Lusk, the Westons and McAllisters at Turvey, the Taylors at Swords, Jim Lawless at Cloughren and the Dukes at St Margaret's. The point of mobilisation was to be at Knocksedan near Swords.

While many Volunteers grabbed their weapons and equipment and prepared to mobilise, others were suspicious of the order and chose to ignore the call to arms believing that it was another false alarm.

As Dr Hayes made his way towards the assembly point he called into the local post office. The postmistress informed him that she had just delivered a wire code from Dublin Castle to the police sergeant at Lusk. She was familiar with the code and said that the message ordered the sergeant to arrest Ashe and Dr Hayes immediately. Dr Hayes hastened his pace towards Knocksedan.[3]

Located on the old northern coach road from Dublin to Belfast, Knocksedan lies two miles west of Swords where the Dublin to Ballymun road crosses the Ward River.

The turnout at Knocksedan was much smaller than the previous day. Only half of the Swords Company had mobilised and the other companies only consisted of a few Volunteers. Ashe's force consisted of fewer than sixty Volunteers.

As Patrick Pearse was reading the Proclamation of the Irish Republic from the steps of the General Post Office on Sackville Street, Commandant Ashe addressed his small force, explaining the importance of the day and of their future actions.

Most of the officers were dressed in Volunteer uniform. The remaining ranks wore their equipment, bandolier, haversack and belt over their civilian clothes.

They were armed with a variety of weapons, including long and short Lee-Enfield rifles, Martini-Enfield rifles and Mauser rifles from the Howth landing, and an assortment of revolvers and automatic pistols of various calibres. Among the ranks were also a number of American Winchester single-barrel pump-action shotguns. There were about one hundred rounds of ammunition per rifle, three hundred rounds of cartridges loaded with buckshot per shotgun and thirty rounds per pistol. Explosives consisted of sixty pounds of gelignite and two canister type grenades. While each Volunteer had a bicycle, heavier equipment was carried in Dr Hayes's two-seater motorcar and Frank Lawless's horse and cart.[4]

In Dublin city, the opening shots of the Rising had killed two unarmed Metropolitan Policemen, James O' Brien at the gates of Dublin Castle and Michael Lahiff at St Stephen's Green. The order to withdraw the force from the streets was immediately issued.

At 12.15 hours, the military authorities received a telephone message from the Dublin Metropolitan Police stating that Dublin Castle was being attacked by armed Sinn Féiners. At 12.30 hours a telephone call was received by the general officer commanding the Curragh camp. He was ordered to muster the mobile column.

This piquet of troops was kept in constant readiness in order to quell any military or civilian disorder. Troops were immediately entrained from Kildare to Kingsbridge Station (now Heuston Station).[5]

As Commandant Ashe prepared his unit to move out, he sent Joe Lawless on the Hudson motorcycle to meet up with a demolition squad from the Lusk section. The plan was to destroy the Great Northern Railway Bridge crossing the estuary at Rogerstown between Donabate, Rush and Lusk stations. It was vital to try to halt or delay any British attempt to enter Dublin city using the railways. Charlie Weston and Ned Rooney had previously been briefed on the plan and were waiting for Joseph Lawless at Balheary Avenue.[6] Among the section of Lusk men was Volunteer John McCann, a quarry-man with experience of explosives. When the unit arrived at the viaduct they realised the amount of explosives they had was inadequate for the job in hand. Four men were posted to cover the approaches to the area as the demolition squad set about wiring the bridge.

The gelignite was stacked around the middle girder on the centre pier. It was hoped that by filling the expansion space between the ends of the girders it would create a compression effect and destroy the bridge. McCann prepared the fuse, crimping the detonator with his teeth. Setting a fifteen-minute fuse the Volunteers withdrew to a safe distance. Telegraph lines were cut and as the Volunteers prepared to move out a tremendous explosion shook the embankment as rails and sleepers were catapulted into the air. The explosion, however, only succeeded in dislodging a length of rail.[7]

The squad moved out on their bicycles with Lawless leading the section on Ashe's motorcycle. On the way to Finglas, Lawless had to abandon the motorcycle as it ran out of petrol. The Volunteers continued to cut the telegraph lines as they made their way towards their camp just south of Finglas Village.

On arriving at the camp, a meal of sandwiches and boiled eggs was served to the men.

The camp at Finglas overlooked the northern suburbs of the city and was located on high ground east of the Dublin road. During the day it had been heavily fortified and every approach was covered.

A courier arrived from Volunteer headquarters at the General Post Office with orders stating that the 5th Battalion were to move to Finglas, hold the main road and engage any enemy officers returning by that route from the Fairyhouse Races. Rifle pits were dug near the roadway and concealed with undergrowth. Volunteers took up position and waited. No British soldiers returned by the road, and as the evening wore on sentries were posted and relieved at regular intervals.

The British Army made use of the railway infrastructure and Colonel Portal arrived at Kingsbridge railway station (now Heuston Station) in Dublin city with the advance guard of the Curragh Mobile Column from County Kildare. Portal's 3rd Reserve Cavalry Brigade consisted of one thousand five hundred armed troops made up of soldiers of the 8th Reserve Cavalry regiment (16th/17th Lancers, King Edward's Horse, Dorsetshire, Oxfordshire Yeomanry); 9th Reserve Cavalry regiment (3rd/7th Hussars, 2nd/3rd County of London Yeomanry); 10th Reserve Cavalry regiment (4th/ 8th Hussars, Lancashire Hussars, Duke of Lancasters/Westmorland/Cumberland Yeomanry). The British troops were being mobilised throughout the country and in England, Major General A.E. Sandbach, C.B., D.S.O., received orders to mobilise the 59th North Midland Division and move immediately to Ireland.

That night a light rain descended on the Volunteer encampment at Finglas. The Volunteers huddled together, as the only shelter was a dilapidated cowshed, which was already over-crowded with men. Morale remained high as the Volunteers learned through their despatch carrier, Molly Adrian, of the declaration of a republic, the occupation of the General Post Office and the seizure of strategic points throughout the city. Many of the men bedded down in the open and were soon asleep.

Commandant Ashe, Adjutant Hayes and Quartermaster Frank Lawless held an officer briefing and decided on their next course of action. It was decided to destroy the railway infrastructure at Blanchardstown. Ashe detailed a section of twenty-two Volunteers for the operation. The men gathered their equipment and checked their weapons. At 22.00 hours, Captain Richard Coleman led the section out of the camp and the Volunteers rode out in to the darkness of the night.

Before retiring for the night, Commandant Ashe toured the camp, talking to the Volunteers. Drawn from all walks of life and all corners of North County Dublin, together the battalion demonstrated the unity, sense of patriotic duty and local pride that marked the general spirit of the day. An independent Irish Republic had been declared, and in the next few days, Ashe knew, his battalion would be called upon to defend their newly acquired independence. But at what cost?

Chapter 3

Tuesday 25 April 1916

Brigadier General W.H.M. Lowe, commanding the Reserve Cavalry Brigade at the Curragh, arrived at Kingsbridge Station at 03.45 hours with the leading troops from the 25th Irish Reserve Infantry Brigade, and assumed command of the forces in the Dublin area, which were roughly two thousand three hundred men of the Dublin garrison, the Curragh mobile column of one thousand five hundred dismounted cavalrymen and eight hundred and forty men of the 25th Irish Reserve Infantry Brigade.[1]

The British Army were reinforcing their positions in Dublin city by entraining troops from depots throughout the country. The plan to retake the metropolis had commenced. It was vital for the Volunteers to disrupt this source of entry into Dublin city.

The Volunteer section that had headed to Blanchardstown was not very familiar with the roads, and soon the party got lost. Having decided to abandon the mission, the Volunteers returned to camp and settled down to try and get some sleep before reveille.

As the camp awoke the next morning, many of the men washed in a nearby stream.

For breakfast, Joe Taylor killed a sheep and the Volunteers had a meal of mutton, eggs, tea and bread. The cooking utensils and rations were distributed from the quartermaster's horse van that was driven by Volunteer Bill Norton. After eating, the Volunteers cleaned and checked their weapons. Bicycles were also cleaned and maintained.

Earlier that morning Commandant Ashe sent Miss Molly Adrian, who was acting as a runner, to Volunteer headquarters at the General Post Office with a report on the battalion's position, numbers and armaments. The messenger returned with instructions from Commandant James Connolly requesting that Ashe send forty men to headquarters. Commandant Ashe could only afford to send twenty and he again detailed Captain Richard Coleman to lead the group. Within twenty-four hours part of this group would be in action against Crown forces at the Mendicity Institute.[2] As they left camp many of the Volunteers were disappointed, as they had all deduced that the city battalions had failed to turn out in strength. The 5th Battalion was seriously reduced in numbers but the men's spirits remained high.

The order also requested that the 5th Battalion engage in diversionary raids. They were detailed to sabotage and generally harass government forces, cut their communications and supplies and perform hit-and-run attacks. It was hoped that these commando operations would relieve pressure on Volunteer positions in Dublin city.

At 11.00 hours Lieutenant Richard Mulcahy and two Volunteers – Tom Maxwell and Paddy Grant – entered the camp.[3] They had been cut off from their city unit and heard that Ashe's battalion was in the area. Lieutenant Richard (Dick) Mulcahy was thirty years old. Born in Manor Street, County Waterford, Mulcahy joined the Post Office Engineering Department in 1902. He was a member of the Irish Volunteers since its formation in 1913 and was also a member of the Irish Republican Brotherhood and the Gaelic League. It was through these organisations that Commandant Ashe knew him. Richard Mulcahy was a calm and collected individual with a mind for military planning and organisation. He was dressed in a Volunteer uniform and carried a Mauser automatic pistol. Commandant Ashe realised Mulcahy's potential and appointed him second in command.

In the afternoon a steady rain began to fall. The Volunteers commandeered a number of sacks from a nearby farm. They draped them around their shoulders and huddled together as the rain pelted down.

That evening the depleted battalion moved to new billets near Knocksedan and bivouacked for the night at a deserted farmhouse at Killeek. The farmhouse still possessed some roofing and was dry inside. Others billeted in the outhouses where they bedded down on straw in the sheds. The men collapsed, exhausted, onto the floor. Outside, Commandant Ashe posted sentries that covered all approaches to their camp.

At Knocksedan they were joined by a number of Volunteers from the 1st Battalion that had escaped being cut off by the British Army at Phibsboro in Dublin city. Volunteers Gerry Golden, Paddy Holohan, Peader and Tom Blanchfield, Anthony

O'Reilly and Willie Walsh marched into the camp. It materialised that after their position on the North Circular Road came under sustained artillery fire, the unit pulled back and were cut off from the 1st Battalion area of the Four Courts.[4] They made their way northwards, resting briefly in Glasnevin Cemetery. A passing British patrol discovered the Volunteers and a gunbattle commenced. Taking cover behind the headstones the Volunteers returned fire. Soon, it began to rain heavily. Using the downpour as cover, the Volunteers fell back through the graveyard, wading across the River Tolka and headed northwards, keeping to the fields and ditches in order to avoid British patrols. They asked at a number of places the whereabouts of Ashe's battalion. Finally, after travelling for hours, the exhausted and hungry men arrived at the camp.[19]

Commandant Ashe held a briefing with his officers, and the area for operations was to be Swords in North County Dublin. It was decided to attack the police barracks at Swords and Donabate the following morning. A plan of action was discussed before the officers retired.

That night, the Volunteers could clearly hear the sound of gunfire emanating from Dublin city.

Chapter 4

Wednesday 26 April 1916

Early on Wednesday morning, Commandant Ashe announced that the battalion was to be organised in to a mobile tactical unit. This combat force was to be divided into four fighting columns. The whole unit comprised of fifty-one men including officers. There were to be four sections of eleven to twelve men, with one junior officer in command of each section and with the four remaining officers comprising the headquarters staff. Ashe explained to the men that he wanted each section to work as a complete entity.

The routine for future engagements would be as follows:

One section would make up the advance guard (point position);
The second section would contain the main body that would include the commanding officer and battalion staff;

The third section would act as the rearguard; and
The fourth section would remain in camp, securing the encampment and carrying out fatigue duties.
These section duties would alternate on a daily basis. The junior officers commanding the sections were: Section One: Charlie Weston; Section Two: Joe Lawless; Section Three: Ned Rooney; and Section Four: Jim Lawless.[1]

There were more additions to the unit as James Kelly, Peter Ganly and Jack McGowan cycled into the camp.[2] Commandant Ashe told a crestfallen Jack McGowan to go home as he was too young. The others were given weapons and ammunition, and were allotted to a section.

At 08.30 hours, three sections moved out of the camp with the objective of capturing Swords and Donabate police barracks and destroying communications within the area.

The three sections made their way towards Swords Village. Each section was well dispersed with the riders travelling in pairs. As they approached the outskirts of the village a motorcyclist drove by at high speed. The first two sections were taken by surprise as the rider sped past. Volunteer Michael McAllister, with the rear section, managed to fire a shot at the rider but he drove on. The Volunteers suspected that the rider was scouting for the British forces.[3]

Joseph Lawless led the advance guard and cycled directly into the centre of Swords village, passing the R.I.C. barracks. Sergeant O'Reilly stood at the doorway, his tunic unbuttoned and his hands in his trouser pockets. He watched with curiosity as the Volunteers cycled through the town. Dismounting from their bicycles in Chapel Lane, the Volunteers spread out and prepared their assault. Eight Volunteers moved rapidly towards the wood at the rear of the barracks. One Volunteer went to meet Section Two and report on the situation to Ashe. Lawless and two Volunteers watched the front of the building. The barracks was not in a state of defence as the loop-holed steel plate shutters were open and the reinforced door stood ajar. Lawless, his rifle hanging from his shoulder, walked towards the sergeant and bid him a good morning. The sergeant, used to seeing the Volunteers 'playing at soldiers', returned the greeting. Lawless walked on by and took up position at a butcher's shop. He watched as his other two men covered the front of the building from the street opposite. Within ten minutes Section Two and Section Three swept into the village and in an orderly manner the police barracks was rushed. The sergeant was taken by surprise as Section Two stormed the station. Six policemen were kept under armed guard as the Volunteers moved from room to room searching for arms and ammunition. A number of revolvers, carbines and ammunition were seized. Lawless took a box containing revolver ammunition and was surprised to find that some of the packages contained cylindrical flat-headed bullets of the dumdum type, illegal under the articles of war.[4]

Meanwhile, Section Three made their way to the post office and began destroying the telegraph. Phone lines were also cut throughout the village.

A party from Section Four arrived in the village and began foraging for supplies. To their delight a motorised bread van drove into the village. Immediately, the vehicle and its contents of freshly baked bread from Kennedy's Bakery were commandeered. Paddy Grant knew how to drive a van and it was taken back to camp at Killeek under escort.

The battalion moved out towards Donabate village with Charlie Weston's section taking point position. Bennie McAllister knew the layout of the village and the position of the barracks. It was decided to adopt the same plan that was used in Swords. Two sections remained outside the village near the railway bridge, securing the perimeter of the village and preparing the railway tracks and telegraph poles for demolition. Here, shots were fired at a man who refused to halt. With the police barracks only two hundred yards way, the shots alerted the garrison who immediately put the building in a state of defence. Lieutenant Mulcahy berated the men for having lost the element of surprise.

Commandant Ashe and Mulcahy entered the village with Weston's section. Entering the post office, Ashe and Mulcahy dismantled the telephone and telegraph equipment. The postmaster, an ex-R.I.C. constable, offered to negotiate the surr-ender of the barracks. Commandant Ashe agreed to this and the man was permitted to make his way into the barracks. After a few minutes, he re-emerged from the building and told Ashe that there were two men working in the building and that they should be let out. He also told the commandant that the sergeant refused to surrender the building. Ashe permitted the workmen to leave.

The barracks was fifty yards from the roadway and approached by a gravel path.

Having taken up assault positions, Weston approached the building and demanded the surrender of the police. The answer was a revolver shot fired from behind a steel shutter. Weston took cover as the Volunteers laid down a covering fire that erupted in one simultaneous blaze. Bullets ricocheted off the stone pillars and embedded themselves in the wooden frames of the doors and windows. The police returned fire.

Armed with a pickaxe, sledgehammer and crowbar, Weston and six men dashed across the fire-strewn ground towards the bolted door of the police station. They battered furiously at the door and it soon gave way. Inside the hallway, they were confronted with another door of steel. They immediately began battering this door until the frame gave way. However, the Volunteers were unable to gain entry as the debris from the door hindered their advance.

On hearing the sound of gunfire, Commandant Ashe reacted quickly and moved reinforcements into the village. The shooting suddenly stopped and a white handkerchief was poked through the shuttering.

The barracks surrounded and the situation hopeless, the policemen decided to surrender. Charlie Weston covered the policemen with his rifle as they vacated the barracks. One of the constables had received a gunshot wound to the hand. The Volunteers quickly cleared the barracks of weapons and ammunition, and the wounded policeman had his hand dressed. Ashe ordered some of his men to remove the imperial coat of arms from the front of the building. A tricolour flag was tied to a brush handle and flown from the roof of the station.[5]

Commandant Ashe took the day book from the barracks. He pointed out entries detailing the names and addresses of local Volunteers and information on parades. As before, the police were released with a warning from Commandant Ashe not to take up arms against the new Irish Republic.

Nearby, Joe Lawless and Bartle Weston set about destroying the railway tracks while others from the section rendered the switch points and junction switches unserviceable.

Before they pulled out of the village, food was purchased from a local shop, which was paid for by Ashe. Having completed their mission each section moved out and returned to camp. After eating a hearty meal, the Volunteers lay out on the grass, talking about the day's events. Molly Adrian arrived from the General Post Office with a copy of the Proclamation of the Republic and a copy of the *Irish War News*. She reported on the situation in Dublin city. British troops were in action against the newly declared republic. Some of the Volunteers realised that the Rising was not going as expected, with only Dublin in rebellion. Another addition to the battalion was the arrival of Mick Fleming from Drumcondra.

That night Commandant Ashe, Lieutenant Mulcahy and Adjutant Hayes reflected on the day's events. For most of the young Volunteers, the actions had been their first engagement in real combat situations. The officers were impressed with the rapid movement of each section. The following day, it was planned to attack Garristown village with the object of capturing Garristown Post Office and police barracks.

Chapter 5

Thursday 27 April 1916

At 02.00 hours three sections moved out to attack Garristown R.I.C. station. Two sections secured the outskirts of the village. The main section moved into the village and surrounded the barracks. The police were called on to surrender. However, the Volunteers discovered that many of the constables had been withdrawn to Balbriggan and only one constable remained in the barracks. The Volunteers searched the building and found no munitions. Lieutenant Dick Mulcahy and some Volunteers raided the post office. The telegraph equipment and telephone were put beyond use. Lieutenant Mulcahy also took what money was in the office as it had been decided by Volunteer command that British Government money constituted 'spoils of war'. Mulcahy gave the postmaster a receipt for the money that he had taken.[1]

The Volunteers moved on to billets at Baldwinstown near Garristown. Here they were joined by Section Four, and the defensive preparations of the camp began. Sentries were positioned to achieve the best field of fire if the camp came under attack. The others occupied old stables and settled down for some sleep.

Later that morning the officers were confronted by a number of men who were complaining that the country had not risen in rebellion. They stated that the executive council had not authorised the Rising and they were acting contrary to their orders from Eoin MacNeill. Commandant Ashe paraded the battalion and told them that the rest of the country had not risen, but that they would. They, the 5th Battalion, were an example of what could be achieved. He stated that he was not going to keep any man against his will and those who wanted to were free to leave. Commandant Ashe addressed every section individually and asked them if they wanted to continue. Every man of the section shouted 'Fight on.'[2] Only two men withdrew from the ranks. They handed in their weapons and left the camp.

Commandant Ashe knew that the days ahead were going to be difficult and that Bill Norton, because of his age, could not cope with the vigorous regime that lay ahead. It was decided to send Bill home, and with great disappointment he left the camp.

Father Kelvehan, the son of an old Fenian, arrived at the camp and requested to bless the Volunteers. The battalion knelt down and the priest administered a blessing, asking God to watch over and protect the men in the days ahead.

At 14.00 hours the battalion moved southwards and bivouacked at Borranstown between Garristown and Ashbourne. Here an old farmhouse provided shelter. The Volunteers set about making the building more habitable. Having posted guards, fires were lit and food was cooked. Many of the

Volunteers were unfamiliar with the area and a number of reconnaissance patrols went out during the day to familiarise the sections with the topography of the vicinity.

That night, Commandant Ashe, Lieutenant Mulcahy, Adjutant Hayes and B.Q.M.S. Lawless sat at a small table in the farmhouse. Illuminated by the light of a candle, the officers discussed the plan of action for the following day. It was planned to attack the Midland Great Western Railway near Batterstown about ten miles from the camp.

Intelligence reports that had been received stated that British troops with field artillery were travelling towards Dublin. It was vital to try to stop or delay any military transports that were using the railway lines. The officers began to fix the details of the scheme of manoeuvre and attack in their minds.

Morale was high among the men. Many talked, joked and reminisced on the last few days' actions. To the delight of all present, Paddy Brogan broke into song, singing 'Doran's Ass'. A rapturous applause at the end resounded through the camp. The camp settled down and many men turned in for the night. In four days of activity the Fingal force seems to have been ignored by the enemy, who no doubt had their hands full in Dublin. That situation, however, was about to change.

***

At Slane in County Meath, County Inspector Alexander 'Baby' Gray of the Royal Irish Constabulary had been receiving reports stating that a number of police barracks had been attacked. Intelligence reports for County Meath for the month of April had stated that there was no dissident activity in the area and that the local populace were law-abiding citizens.[3] Three barracks had been attacked in North County Dublin in as many days and Gray believed that the police barracks in County Meath were under threat. County Inspector Gray was an officer with thirty-three years of service. He had served in Dingle, County Kerry, during the period of the Land War in the 1880s. He was notorious for his acts of repression on behalf of the local landlords and it was during this turbulent period that the police officer got the nickname 'Baby Gray' because of his boyish looks.[4]

In County Meath there were thirty-six R.I.C. stations. While many were mere huts, others were fortified two-storey houses. The inspector decided to abandon the smaller posts and reinforce the bigger barracks. He also decided to organise a mobile 'Quick Reaction Force' that could, at speed, intercept those responsible for attacking the stations. He immediately began to gather a force of armed constables from throughout the district. He drew men from Navan, Trim, Kells, Oldcastle, Athboy, Dunshaughlin, Nobber, Duleek, Dunboyne, Summer-hill, Ballivor, Moynalty, Crossakiel, Carnaross, Bohermeen, Drumconrath, Longwood, Lismullin, Enfield, Kilmoon, Killyon, Carlanstown, Oristown, Kilmainhamwood, Robinstown, Ballinabrackey, Moyglare, Stirrupstown, George Cross, Parsonstown, Julianstown, Gormanston, Ticoghan and Ashbourne. They assembled in Slane, County Meath.

He appointed District Inspector Harry Smyth from Navan as his second in command. Inspector Smyth originally came from Herefordshire, England, and had sixteen years' service in the Constabulary. He also had previous service as an officer in the British Army. Stationed in Navan since 1912, Smyth was an experienced officer.

Transport for the force was arranged by commandeering seventeen motor vehicles from the local gentry. Due to the lack of police drivers, a number of men with relevant driving experience were pressed into service. The two police officers inspected their men. The force consisted of fifty-four armed constables. They were armed with Lee-Enfield, Mark I Carbines that had been sighted up to two thousand yards. Many also carried Webley revolvers and each constable wore a bandolier full of .303 ammunition.

County Inspector Alexander Gray's force was ready for rapid deployment as the occasion might demand. That occasion was only a matter of hours away.

Chapter 6

Friday 28 April 1916: Morning

At 10.30 hours on Friday morning, three Volunteer sections moved out from the camp and cycled towards the crossing of the main Dublin to Slane road. The mission was to attack the Midland Great Western Railway near Batterstown. In total there were thirty-six volunteers and three officers. Number One Section was led by Charlie Weston, which formed the advance guard. Ned Rooney commanded Number Two Section that made up the main body. Section leader Joe Lawless made up the rearguard with Number Three Section. The quartermaster, Frank Lawless, and Number Four Section were to remain in camp. The day was dry with bright sunshine, warm with a slight breeze, as the Volunteers cycled towards their objective.

A recce of the area revealed that the Ashbourne R.I.C. barracks was occupied and threatened the Volunteers' line of withdrawal from their mission at Batterstown. It was decided to attack and take the barracks before they launched an attack on the railway infrastructure.

The barracks was situated one hundred and sixty yards on the southeast side of the Cross of Rath, on the main Dublin to Slane Road, about half a mile north of the village of Ashbourne, County Meath. The building was a detached two-storey dwelling, consisting of a front and rear entry with windows on both sides of the barracks. There were no windows on the gable ends.[1] Defences consisted of reinforced steel doors and metal shuttering on the windows. The sergeants' married quarters formed part of the building, with a separate porch entrance of wood and lattice iron work at the rear. Unknown to the Volunteers, the barracks had already been reinforced and was heavily defended. Having received information that forces of Irish Volunteers were active in the area, security at the barracks had been stepped up. The garrison in the barracks had been reinforced the night before with men from Navan, Dunboyne and Slane and was now commanded by Inspector McCormack. Weapons had been checked and extra ammunition issued to each officer. The barrack sergeant, R.M. Tully, had also set up a perimeter defence on the by-road in the form of a checkpoint manned by three constables.[2]

Charlie Weston's section, riding 'point', approached their objective cautiously, with scouts moving ahead of the lead section, watching and listening. Reaching a bend on the by-road about a quarter of a mile from the junction, the scouts discovered that an improvised roadblock had been erected by the three armed constables manning the perimeter defence. Reporting back to Section Leader Weston, the advance guard stacked their bicycles on the by-road north of the cross. Using the hedgerows and ditches for cover, the Volunteers managed to approach the roadblock unseen. Volunteers Mick McAllister and Jerry Golden rushed the guards. McAllister covered two officers with his rifle but the third, Sergeant Brady of Dunshaughlin, recognised Golden and shouted 'Golden, I'll get you before I die.'[3]

The sergeant drew his revolver and prepared to take aim. Golden raised his rifle but the weapon jammed. Dropping the gun Golden charged forward and grabbed hold of Brady around the waist. Golden was of a small stature and the burly policeman swung the Volunteer around in an attempt to break free. Volunteer Bartle Weston rushed forward and struck the sergeant on the head a number of times with his rifle butt. The constable collapsed to the ground shouting, 'Don't kill me!' The policemen were taken prisoner but during the fracas one constable managed to escape, running away across the fields and hiding in a nearby cottage. The remaining prisoners were marched to the rear and kept under guard.

Commandant Ashe and Lieutenant Mulcahy arrived with Number Two Section. Having been briefed of the situation, they immediately began to disperse their forces in preparation for the assault on the barracks.

The terrain north and south of the building was one of high hedges and ditches that ran parallel to the roads. The landscape provided excellent cover and concealment for the approaching force. Charlie Weston's section moved forward, and using the hedges and ditches for cover took up position at the front of the barracks behind a high bank with a thorn hedge (A). Number Two Section under Ned Rooney and the rearguard under Joe Lawless were ordered to take up position at the rear of the building (B). Here, the lush vegetation shielded the Volunteers' movements. Lieutenant Mulcahy posted two Volunteers, Christy Nugent and James O'Connor at the Rath Crossroads in order to cover the approaches to the police station.

Ashe walked towards the front of the building and, standing on a high bank by the roadway, he demanded the surrender of the barracks. The request was greeted by a sharp report of gunfire that hit the roadway a few inches from his feet. Ashe dived for cover as Weston's section opened fire. The front of the building was hit by a hail of bullets that splintered the woodwork and tore into the metal shuttering with a dreadful sound that resembled a very loud whip crack. Inside the barracks the constables were firing from all positions fronting the roadway. The flashing muzzles of the police carbines were visible through the slits of the steel shuttering that protected the windows. Cartridge cases soon littered the floor and the rooms filled with the smell of cordite. Sergeant Tully ordered his men to stand firm and continue firing.

Ashe knew that a frontal assault was out of the question, but the building had to be taken. Lieutenant Mulcahy drew his automatic pistol, and with the battalion grenadier, Peader Blanchfield, they moved forward to the top of the ditch. Both men dashed across the bullet-swept roadway in an attempt to get near the barracks. Taking cover behind the hedging and fence that surrounded the station, Lieutenant Mulcahy gave covering fire as Blanchfield primed a canister bomb and lit its fuse. A professional, he took his time, dwelling carefully on the aim. He lobbed the bomb towards the building. The missile flew true and then there was silence. The bomb landed in the centre of the garden fronting the barracks. As the fuse expired there was a tremendous explosion as sods of earth, stone and cabbage stalks were hurled into the air. As the dust and smoke cleared the Volunteers saw that the building was undamaged. They opened a rapid fire and renewed their attack with vigour.

The heavy rate of fire from the barracks had dwindled to sporadic single shots. The psychological impact of the explosion on the beleaguered garrison soon resulted in the hoisting of a white flag from an upper window of the building.

Ashe ordered the police to come out with their hands on their heads and warned that if there was any treachery he would order his men to open fire. As the door opened and the police emerged, everyone heard the sound of a car horn and a single shot rang out from the direction of the crossroads. The police immediately turned and ran back inside the barracks, locking the door. Looking towards the junction, the Volunteers saw that a convoy of black cars was approaching at speed. Ashe shouted to his men 'Stop those cars!'

Chapter 7

Friday 28 April 1916: Early Afternoon

From a vantage point on Limekiln Hill overlooking the Slane to Ashbourne Road, local men John Austin, Matt Gargan and George Stafford watched as the Volunteers launched their attack on the barracks.

Turning their gaze towards the crossroads they noticed that the two Volunteers who had been posted as sentries to watch the northwest side of the crossroads had become preoccupied with the events at the barracks and had failed to notice a number of police vehicles approaching at speed. The spectators watched as Volunteer Christy Nugent turned and fired a shot at the approaching vehicles from his Martini Carbine before it jammed. The single gunshot alerted the Volunteers and brought the convoy to a halt. The two Volunteers quickly withdrew and made their way towards Joe Lawless and his section at the rear of the barracks.

Earlier that morning, Inspector Alexander Gray had received information that a large party of rebels were marching on Ashbourne. At 11.00 hours his 'flying squad' left Slane and drove at high speed towards Ashbourne village. The constables sat in the vehicles with their rifles across their knees, their helmets resting on the butts of the weapons. Each man was an experienced officer and confidence abounded that this insurrection would be put down just like all the rest. Inspector Gray's vehicle led the convoy as they drove out of Slane. District Inspector Smyth sat beside Constable Eugene Bratton, who drove the last vehicle in the convoy. As the convoy reached a point above Kilmoon, Inspector Smyth ordered his driver to stop. Smyth spoke to a local man who pointed with his hand and said 'They,' meaning the rebels, 'are along the road'.[1] Smyth tried desperately to catch up with the rest of the convoy to warn them, but as they neared the Rath Crossroads a single shot rang out forcing the column of vehicles to a standstill.

On hearing the report of a rifle and the car horn, Ashe prepared to withdraw his force. Mulcahy, however, urged the commander to hold the position. Two men were detailed to cover the front of the police barracks and fire occasionally to keep the police holed up inside. Mulcahy ordered Charlie Weston to carry out a recce on the crossroads. The Volunteer returned within minutes and reported that there was a large force of police, estimated at about one hundred. Mulcahy said, 'It does not matter if there is a thousand, we will deal with those fellows.' He went on, 'Get your men along the road to the cross and keep them under fire and don't waste ammunition. I know you are good fellows. I will get round them with the rest of the main body. You hold on to the crossroads.'[2]

Weston called his squad together. Paddy Doyle and John McAllister covered the Volunteers as they moved into position on the roadway. Moving at the double, using the hedges and ditches for cover, Section Leader Charlie Weston, along with his brother Bartle Weston and Bennie McAllister, took up position on the bank on the right-hand side of the road. Jerry Golden, Dick Aungier and Mick McAllister took up position on the left-hand side of the road. As the vehicles drew to a halt, Weston's squad took careful aim and opened fire.

The leading five cars took the brunt of Weston's section's assault. The sound of splintering glass intertwined with the metallic ping of bullets impacting on metal was deafening as bullets ripped through the vehicles, around the heads and bodies of the police officers. The first car slewed to a standstill as it drove into the storm of gunfire. Inspector Gray ordered his command to dismount and fight on foot. As the rest of the convoy came to a halt and the police debussed from their vehicles, they were engulfed by a murderous barrage of bullets.

The noise was deafening and there was pandemonium among the police as one car after another drove into range. As the police left their vehicles, many attempted to don their helmets while others dropped their rifles and ran for cover. The police fired back into the maelstrom but those who failed to run for cover were soon shot dead or wounded. As Inspector Gray stood by the leading vehicle, ordering his men to take cover and establish a defensive area, he was hit by a burst of gunfire. Both his hands were shattered by blasts from a shotgun and he was also wounded in the upper body. He stumbled for cover into the ditch alongside the road.

Having left the vehicles, many had made a collective rush from the cars towards the right-hand side of the road. Some of the men who emerged from the cars managed to follow their wounded inspector and crawl to safety in the roadside ditch, from where they returned fire in a bid to take out the insurgent gunmen.

Bullets hit home, shearing through flesh, smashing and splintering bone. Clots of mud, shreds of uniform and broken rifles exploded into the air. The bodies of the men pitched off the road into the ditch. The Volunteers watched as one figure crawled over the roadway like a worm, leaving a trail of blood behind him, and finally tumbled into a hollow.

Constable James Gormley was shot dead as he attempted to return fire. He was twenty-five years old and had almost four years of service in the force. Leaving a vehicle, Sergeant John Shanagher made an attempt to cross the road and came into the sights of Volunteer Mick McAllister. Squeezing the trigger of his rifle McAllister saw the police constable keel over as the bullets found their target. Sergeant John Shanagher was a native of County Roscommon and was forty-eight years old with over twenty-five years of service. Constable Richard McHale was next to be hit and he slumped dead on the roadway. He was twenty-two years old and had three years of service in the Constabulary.

For those constables caught in the open, it was a terrifying experience. Many lay wounded on the road in full view of the Volunteers, unable to make the drainage ditches on either side of the roadway. From the cover of the gully at the side of the road, the wounded County Inspector Gray ordered his men to provide covering fire so the remainder could get off the road. The gunfire was so intense this proved almost impossible. Others who failed to make the ditch sought cover beneath the cars. In an attempt to cover his colleagues caught in the open, Constable Michael Jo Duggan took up position beneath one of the leading vehicles. He opened fire on Weston's position.

Reloading his weapon, he continued to pour fire towards the Volunteers at the crossroads. Puffs of dust were thrown up as Volunteer rounds peppered the ground inches from the constable's head.[3] As the police tried to regain control, all they could hear was the fiendish whine of the bullets and the sobbing groans of their wounded comrades. Shouts for medical assistance echoed through the air.

After the initial burst of heavy fire that pinned the police down, Weston's men calmly set about picking their targets. Any sign of movement came under fire. From his concealed position, Section Leader Weston received an order from Commandant Ashe to disengage and withdraw. Weston signalled to his squad to move out. As Weston pulled back and moved along a drainage channel towards the barracks, a runner arrived with another order: to go back and hold their original position. Returning to the ditch, the section managed to occupy the same position. The police positions had not changed. Once again they commenced firing.

Having been confronted by a large force, Ashe again planned to pull his men out and had ordered the withdrawal of Weston's section. Mulcahy had rushed back to the Commandant's position near the barracks and urged him not to withdraw but to press home the attack. Mulcahy assured Ashe that with the tactic of surprise and mobility the police could be defeated. The Volunteers were to hold the line.

Behind the barracks Numbers Two and Three Sections were in a quandary as what to do. Section Leaders Lawless and Rooney decided to fall back to area (C). Looking across the fields towards the barracks Lawless noticed Mulcahy moving in their direction, evidently looking for the two sections. As Mulcahy raced towards their position, bullet rounds kicked up sods of clay and stone around him. Having arrived unscathed, the lieutenant ordered the two sections to follow him to the Garristown Road (F). Two Volunteers were ordered to cover the rear of the barracks while Dr Hayes occupied a nearby cottage and established a medical post (H).

Mulcahy planned to exploit the mayhem by sending two of his sections into action. He assured the men that the police did not have a chance and that the plan was to rout or capture the entire force.[4] From the Garristown Road, Section Two was to provide support fire for Weston's unit, who were holding the crossroads. Section Three, commanded by Lawless, would make their way to the rear of the police convoy (D). Here they would wait until an attack was launched from the crossroads, their mission being to trap the police and prevent them from escaping.

Section Leader Ned Rooney ordered his men into position. The squad sprinted to a ditch on the opposite side of the Garristown Road and took up firing positions (F) and (G). Weapons were locked and loaded and trained towards the police positions.

Ashe appeared and Mulcahy briefed him of the plan. Ashe nodded in approval and stated that he would lead Lawless and his section to the rear of the police convoy, as he knew the area well. As the unit moved out, the order to 'open fire' was given to Rooney's section. The tree line erupted in a massive wall of gunfire as his squad laid down covering fire.

Mulcahy had arranged small squads of Volunteers into positions that would allow the Volunteers to fire into the ranks of the police. Rushing them back and forth across the field of battle would create an impression of strength.

The constables returned fire at extremely close quarters in order to hold their ground in what had become a confused and brutal melee. Cartridge cases littered the bottom of the ditch and uniforms had become smeared with dirt and cordite. Others were covered in blood, their own and that of their colleagues. The number of wounded in the ditch began to increase. An officer shot through the leg had a tourniquet applied to limit the bleeding. Others lay face down in the ditch, some silent, others moaning. Those who failed to make the ditch or the cars had scattered and hit the ground after the initial shots. Exposed and under fire, they tried to find cover from which to return fire. The dead bodies of their fallen comrades provided some cover. Crawling on their bellies they manoeuvred into better firing positions. Lying prone in the centre of the road they fired back towards the crossroads where Weston's section was entrenched. The Volunteers soon identified the targets and fired back. Working the bolts of their rifles furiously, they succeeded in silencing a number of the constables on the roadway.[5]

Constable James Hickey was shot dead. He was forty-nine years old and had almost twenty-six years of service. Many others had been seriously wounded and lay silent. The civilian chauffeurs were shot in the driving seats of their vehicles. Their bodies slumped over the steering wheels or hung out the half opened doors of the cars.

The battle, which had lasted about one and a half hours at this point, was draining for both sides. The physical exertion, the fear and concentration required, were all taking their toll. There was also the constant assault on a man's senses: the relentless noise, the shouting, the screams of the wounded, the yelling of commands, the rip of pistol fire, the snap of rifles and the boom of the shotguns all contributed to the confusion of battle.

The badly wounded County Inspector Gray continued to command the police near the crossroads. The number of incoming rounds was intense. Many of his men had been caught in the open. Running the gauntlet to cover, many had seen the flashes of rifle fire through the hedging that cut through their ranks. The police were now taking fire from the Rath Crossroads and enfilading fire from across the field at the Garristown Road (F) and (G). Dozens of Volunteer muzzle flashes emanated from the hedges and the tree line. Inspector Gray tried desperately to find out where the enemy was entrenched. The wounded police on the road were in a desperate plight but could not be reached through the gunfire, which opened up every time someone tried.

Inspector Smyth commanded the police detachment at the end of the column and they could hear the firing further up the convoy. Having bailed out of the cars, Smyth had established a perimeter defensive position in the ditches. The thick roadside bush had screened his section. Rounds were coming through the vehicles and also through the trees above their heads. Though not under immediate fire, he could hear Inspector Gray's squad engaging the enemy. He looked at his men: the fear of the impending battle was ingrained on their faces. He checked his revolver and ordered his men to make ready. It would only be a matter of time.

Chapter 8

Friday 28 April, 1916:
Mid-Afternoon

Accompanied by Commandant Ashe, Section Leader Joe Lawless, Peader Blanchfield, Johnny Devine, Paddy Brogan, Jack Rafferty, Jimmy Connor and Nicholas Teeling began their journey towards the rear of the police convoy. Moving parallel to the main road, they used the natural landscape for cover. Keeping low and moving in Indian file (single file) they entered the fields and began moving towards the Dublin to Slane Road. As they crept silently along, the bushes and trees screened their advance. In order to get to the road unseen, they pushed forwards along the irrigation ditches at the side of the fields. Wading through the foul smelling water, the Volunteers held their weapons waist high in order to keep them dry and ready for action. The men stumbled and fell in the mud, their faces whipped by the low-hanging trees. Briars and brushwood tore at their skin. Streaks of water ran down their faces as they tried not to fall headlong into the mire. No one spoke unless it was necessary, and even then only in tense, hushed whispers. After what seemed like an eternity the Volunteers reached the road and prepared to take up their positions. Ashe gave the squad a quick briefing and ordered Lawless to cover the rear of the police column and to hold his fire for as long as possible. Wishing the young section leader luck, Ashe headed back towards the Garristown Road.

Joe Lawless described the terrain as follows:

The road boundaries are those common to County Meath roads: A low bank, about eighteen inches to two feet high, dividing a wide shallow channel; this bank is gapped at intervals to allow water to drain from the road. The channel is no deeper than the road surface, but is about three to four feet wide and overgrown in patches with long grass and occasional small bushes. Beyond the channel rises a steep bank, four to six feet high, which has a thorn hedge on the field side, and between it and the fields runs a deep and wide ditch, six to seven feet deep and six to seven feet wide at the top.

As Lawless checked his position he was startled by a figure across the roadway, crouching down beside a motorcycle. Lawless took aim, thinking it was a police officer, but the man protested, stating that he was a friend and was looking to warn the Volunteers of the police convoy. Lawless believed that the man was sincere and told him to clear off across the fields.

Before leaving, the man said that his name was Quigley and that he was the County Surveyor for Meath. He disappeared through the hedges and made off.

Lawless deployed Paddy Brogan and Jack Rafferty at the top edge of the bank with a thick thorn hedge for cover. Peader Blanchfield was positioned behind a tree stump. He carried the remaining canister bomb and was ordered to destroy any car that tried to reverse and drive out. Jack Devine took up position at the front of the bank while Jimmy Connor and Nicholas Teeling covered the rear of the party. Lawless reconnoitred the opposite side of the road and found that the bank was too high and did not offer a good firing position. He made his way back to his men and took up position in the ditch.

***

Inspector Smyth raised himself and looked over the brim of the ditch. The coast looked clear and he ordered Constable Bratten to make his way back towards Kilmoon and raise the alarm. Bratten crawled out of the ditch and, using the hedgerows as cover, moved along the roadway. After travelling about two hundred yards he ran into Joe Lawless and his men. As Lawless beckoned him to raise his hands, a barrage of rifle fire cut through the grass and trees towards the Volunteers. The Volunteers dived for cover and Bratten, seizing the chance to escape, ran as fast he could in the direction of Kilmoon. The Volunteers held their fire but on checking his section, Lawless was informed that Volunteer Jack Rafferty had received a serious wound to the head. Rafferty was dragged into cover. Blood pumped from his wound and ran down his face. An improvised

45

dressing in the form of a handkerchief was used to stem the bleeding. Conscious and in great pain the young Volunteer was escorted by Peader Blanchfield back to the Garristown Road to the cottage where Dr Hayes had established a casualty clearing station. Lawless suddenly realised that Volunteer Blanchfield had taken the canister bomb with him and that if there was an attempt to break out by the police, he would be powerless to stop the vehicles. Lawless ordered his section to hold their fire even though incoming fire was hitting his position. Volunteer Paddy Brogan shouted 'I'm hit' and clutched at his stomach. On closer examination, however, it materialised that his large leather belt had stopped the bullet.

With his position compromised, Section Leader Lawless had no alternative but to order his men to engage the enemy and open fire. Each man pulled back the bolt on his rifle, released the safety catch and squeezed the trigger. The hedgerow erupted in a blaze of gunfire. Spreading their fire along the road, the Volunteers managed to hole the petrol tank of the last police vehicle. This action blocked the road, as the police were now unable to reverse and get past their last car.

Though each side was only a few feet from the other, in most cases the tall grass, the hedging and the embankments greatly obstructed visibility. The police and the Volunteers fired at anything that might indicate the presence of an opponent. The Volunteers emptied magazine after magazine in the direction of Inspector Smyth's position. Bullets whined and cracked through the hedges and trees. In order to gain a better firing position, Joe Lawless and Devine moved out onto the road. Kneeling on one knee they opened fire on the police. Lying prone, both men reloaded and stood up to empty another magazine. As they lay down again to reload, incoming bullets kicked up the earth around them. Lawless was blinded momentarily and had to return to the cover of the ditch to clean the dirt from his face. He reloaded his rifle and moved out again to engage the police.

Inspector Smyth and his men waited with perfect calm for each attack, which they met with fire at point blank range from their weapons. Around them, bullets sliced through the undergrowth, splintering bark off trees and ricocheting off the roadway.

Bullets tore into the officers at the ditch, sending them careering backwards. Bloodstains soaked through their dark green uniforms. Helmets lay discarded on the road, as did a number of weapons. Inspector Smyth was wounded three times as he ordered his men to return fire. Reloading his revolver, Smyth directed his men to keep up a rapid fire in order not to be overwhelmed. Sergeant Young of Kilmoon was shot dead at the ditch. He was forty-two years old and had nineteen years of service.

At the Garristown Road, Ned Rooney's section continued to pour down fire towards Inspector Gray's men near the crossroads. The police continued to fire back, but they were hemmed in and pinned down. Section Leader Rooney received a bullet splinter in the eye and had to be assisted back to the medical aid station where his wound was dressed.

Volunteer Thomas Rafferty, who was firing from the Garristown Road, stood on top of the ditch to see if any police constables were advancing on their position through the fields. He was shot and mortally wounded. He too was carried to the Volunteer medical post at the cottage where Dr Hayes worked frantically to save the young man's life.

On the Garristown Road, Ashe and Mulcahy discussed the battle plan. Both officers knew that the situation could change by the minute. Every second was vital and called for quick decisions. Convinced of a possible victory, Ashe ordered Mulcahy to send for Number Four Section, which was back in the camp. Mulcahy sent a runner back to the camp to rouse Quartermaster Frank Lawless and his section.

Chapter 9

Friday 28 April 1916: The Final Hour

Any attempt by the police to break out from the ditch near the crossroads was greeted by a barrage of rifle fire. Rounds cracked through the air as they fought back to hold their position. Inspector Gray, weak from the loss of blood, ordered his men to hold the line and engage with the enemy. Four hours of combat had reduced his force considerably. The dead and wounded lay scattered on the road and in the ditches. The detritus of battle lay all around.

At the far end of the convoy Inspector Smyth had defended his position and fought back resolutely. His men had opened heavy and accurate fire, inflicting casualties on the Volunteers and forcing them to seek cover. Bullets whined and cracked through the brush as Smyth's men engaged with Joe Lawless and his squad.

From his position in the ditch, covering the rear of the convoy, Volunteer Jimmy Connor noticed a movement to the front of his post. He removed the safety catch from his weapon and made ready. He could clearly hear whispered voices and the snapping of twigs. Connor signalled to Lawless, who rushed to the position, and through the dense hedging could see faces at a distance of about twenty yards. Believing that police reinforcements had arrived and were attempting to outflank his position, Lawless ordered his men to fall back. Raising his rifle, he squeezed the trigger and emptied the magazine in the direction of the faces. Fire was quickly returned in his direction and, to his horror, Lawless realised he was out of ammunition. Drawing his revolver he ordered his men to pull back while he kept the enemy's heads down before making his own escape under heavy fire. Devine and Teeling covered the others as they pulled out back along the ditch. In the confusion of the hurried withdrawal, Lawless became separated from his section and he heard shouting. He believed that his unit had been captured by the police and continued on alone towards the Garristown Road. On arrival he briefed Ashe of the situation.

On hearing the battlefield situation report, Ashe believed that his battalion were in danger of being overwhelmed. He turned and headed towards the Rath Crossroads with the intention of ordering a general retreat of his forces.

After organising his split force by crossing and re-crossing fire-torn ground, Mulcahy dashed back across the bullet-swept crest of the field, returning to the Garristown Road. Mulcahy arrived as Joe Lawless was preparing to move out after replenishing his ammunition. The section leader reiterated his story to the lieutenant. Mulcahy turned and said 'that the enemy force was in fact himself and Section Four from the camp that included Frank Lawless', Joe's father. The shouting he believed was the capture of his men was in fact Mulcahy shouting at them to stop firing on his position. The young section leader felt ill as he realised he had almost shot and killed his father.

On hearing that Ashe was to call a retreat, Mulcahy ran down the road after him. Near the crossroads, under the cover of a ditch, Mulcahy explained the false alarm to Ashe and both officers agreed to continue the fight.

At the Garristown Road, the Volunteers were taking heavy fire from the police positions. Volunteer Matthew Kelly was shot through the forearm and Willie Walsh suffered a wound to his fingers. Both men made their way back to the aid station at the cottage.

At the crossroads, Section Leader Weston and his men still held their position and continued to fire into the ranks of the R.I.C. Weston realised that the police had come under attack from the Slane end of the road and were gradually being forced to fight on two fronts. They were also taking enfilading fire from the Garristown Road. Lieutenant Mulcahy moved up the right-hand side of the road towards the crossroads. Over the noise of battle, Mulcahy's voice could be heard shouting to the police, 'Will you surrender? By God if you don't we will give you a dog's death'.[1] The police answered with a fusillade of rifle fire.

Constable Michael Jo Duggan, firing from beneath the police vehicle, recoiled in horror and rolled on his side unconscious. Regaining his senses, he realised he had been hit. A German pin-pointed bullet entered just behind the heart and came out at the top of his shoulder, just shaving the lung.[2] Gasping for breath, he slipped once again into unconsciousness.

The police were now surrounded with no chance of escape. Sections One and Two had the crossroads and the Garristown Road covered. Sections Three and Four had the rear of the convoy and the fields facing the police position covered. It was now or never.

Mulcahy ordered Section One to fix bayonets, and with the words 'up and at them' they charged towards the police position. Firing his automatic Mauser pistol, Mulcahy led the Volunteers as they assaulted across the open ground. The police could offer little resistance against Mulcahy's rapid and ferocious assault. Falling back in disarray, many constables dropped their weapons and surrendered. Others ran and sought shelter in a nearby labourer's cottage.

At the other end of the roadway, B.Q.M.S. Frank Lawless moved forward in the cover of the bushes to look at the short piece of open ground between his position and that of the police positioned in the ditch. Having carefully surveyed the roadway, he decided that the best way to assault was to storm across in a straight line. As soon as B.Q.M.S. Lawless stood up to begin the attack, the police opened fire and a furious exchange of gunfire erupted, ripping leaves from trees all around. Lawless led his men out of the ditch and charged towards Inspector Smyth's position.

On seeing the Volunteers emerging from cover, Inspector Smyth jumped to the top of the ditch and urged his men to get up and fight. The police scrambled out of the ditch and prepared to meet the Volunteer assault head on. Inspector Smyth wheeled around and fired his revolver at Lawless, missing him by inches. The bullet hit and killed Volunteer John Crenigan. The young Volunteer collapsed as he was hit, his rifle falling on

The Royal Irish Constabulary (R.I.C.) c. 1916
(Courtesy of the Garda Museum)

A typical picture of a southern RIC station, in this case Ennistymon in
County Clare (Courtesy of the PSNI Museum)

A typical entrance to a North Dublin village c. 1916
(From the author's collection)

Typical hedgerows from around Ashbourne today
(From the author's collection)

Hedgerows on the Garristown Road today
(From the author's collection)

The Ashbourne Bocage
(From the author's collection)

Thomas Ashe, commander
of the North Dublin
Battalion (The Capuchin
Archive)

Richard Mulcahy, Thomas
Ashe's second-in-command
and later General in the Free
State Army and leading
politician
(Courtesy of P. Delany)

Battalion Quartermaster for
the North Dublin Battalion,
Frank Lawless (Courtesy of
The National Library of
Ireland)

Dr Richard Hayes, medical
officer of the North Dublin
Battalion (Courtesy of The
National Library of Ireland)

RIC District Inspector Harry
Smyth from Navan
(Courtesy of the Garda
Museum)

RIC County Inspector for
Meath, Alexander 'Baby'
Gray (Courtesy of the
Garda Museum)

An RIC grave in Navan,
Meath (Courtesy R. Bateson)

District Inspector Smyth's
grave (Courtesy R. Bateson)

Volunteer John Crenigan who was killed during the battle, he was twenty-one. (Courtesy R. Bateson)

Volunteer Thomas Rafferty who died from his wounds received during the fighting at Ashbourne (Courtesy R. Bateson)

The memorial to the fallen in Ashbourne (From the author's collection)

Section leader Charlie
Weston (Courtesy of the
Weston Family)

JV Lawless in his Volunteer
Uniform c.1916 (Courtesy
of Lt. Col Lawless)

The Mauser bullets that may
have been mistaken for Dumdum rounds after the battle.
(J. Good)

Thomas Ashe under guard
after the Rising, 1916
(The Capuchin Archive)

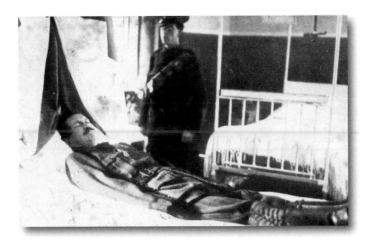

Thomas Ashe lying in state, 1917
(The Capuchin Archive)

A volley of shots fired over Ashe's grave in Glasnevin Cemetery
(The Capuchin Archive)

the roadway. Crenigan was twenty-one years old and came from Roganstown in Swords. He was formerly an employee of the Dublin Tramways Company.

Lawless immediately engaged the approaching police officers emerging from the ditch. Firing his weapon from the hip, Lawless squeezed the trigger and shot Inspector Smyth in the head. The impact of the bullet stopped the advancing police officer, the momentum of the round forcing the body to jerk backwards, brains and bloody fragments of bone shooting in a savage gout onto the ground. The body hit the roadway with a thud, the last gasps of air exiting from his lungs.

On witnessing the death of their officer, the other constables dropped their weapons and raised their hands in surrender. The policemen clambered out of the ditch onto the roadway, their hands held high. An uneasy silence descended as the last shots in the battle were discharged. The Battle of Ashbourne had come to a bloody end.

Chapter 10

Friday 28 April 1916:
Evening

It had been an extraordinarily brutal and bloody battle. Commandant Ashe and Lieutenant Mulcahy walked up the centre of the road. Their boots crunched glass underfoot. The road resembled a charnel house.

Bodies lay where they had fallen, still and contorted or in the last throes of death. The leading cars were riddled with bullet holes. The police officers, invariably at the head of the advancing convoy, were hit badly. At the side of the roadway, there were a large number of slightly wounded constables, while others were unhurt but utterly demoralised.

During the battle, Constable Bratten had evaded capture and had made his way to Kilmoon and continued towards Balrath Barracks. There he had managed to phone Navan and Drogheda

R.I.C. Barracks informing them of the situation at Ashbourne. No police or military force was available to extricate the police at Ashbourne.

Bratten returned to Ashbourne, and as he arrived at the scene of carnage he knew the battle had ended when he saw Inspector Smyth's silver whistle lying on the roadway. The dead bodies of his colleagues had been lined up at the side of the road. Blood and bandages were strewn along the roadside.

Bratten approached Ashe and asked permission to take Inspector Smyth's body home. Ashe agreed and ordered that a car be provided to transport the remains of the D.I. The body was placed on the back seat and Bratten drove to the Inspector's house where his wife, Georgina Eveleen Smyth, received the body. His death left her a widow with four children of between two and fifteen years of age.

During the battle there had been no fire from Ashbourne Police Barracks. Commandant Ashe ordered the constabulary that garrisoned the building to surrender. During the battle they had been kept pinned down by two Volunteers from Number One Section. As they paraded out of the building with their hands above their heads, the Volunteers were surprised to learn that instead of the usual six police officers, the barracks had been reinforced before the battle and fifteen constables under the command of a District Inspector emerged. Commandant Ashe offered the senior surviving police officer a cigarette and assured the officer that his men would be treated well.

Having spent many years in Kerry during the latter part of the nineteenth century, the severely wounded Inspector Gray recognised Ashe's accent and refused the medical assistance offered by the Volunteers. Volunteer Joe Lawless produced a small camera, and with his rifle slung over his shoulder he took some photographs of the aftermath of the battle.

Commandant Ashe ordered his men to collect all the arms and ammunition and to see to the wounded. Many of the wounded constables were taken to the R.I.C. barrack building where Dr Hayes and Molly Adrian treated their wounds, assisted by the Murray girls, who had recently arrived on the scene. Those who had been seriously wounded were treated on the roadside. One policeman who had been travelling in the first vehicle had been very badly wounded. He had four bullets in one leg, one in the thigh and two in the body. He slipped in and out of consciousness as a Volunteer attempted to stem the flow of blood. The constable gestured to a knapsack and asked the Volunteer to take out a flask of whiskey. The policeman asked, 'Is it a sin to drink whiskey when you are dying?' The Volunteer reassured him that it wasn't and offered the flask to the constable. As he sipped the liquid he said, 'It's too bad we have to be fighting one another.' In a few moments he was dead.[1]

As Dr Hayes made his way among those lying on the roadside one of the wounded constables stretched out his arms and impulsively cried, 'Oh, we are all Irishmen. You know me, Sir. You know me. Sir, I am Glennon the boxer.'[2]

The Volunteers sent to Ashbourne for a priest to give spiritual assistance to the dying and to administer the last rites to those who were already dead. Father Murphy and Father Dillon arrived. They were very hostile to the Volunteers and paraded up and down the road calling them 'murderers'.[3]

A number of the civilian drivers had also been killed or wounded. Albert Kepp, the chauffeur for the Marchioness of Conyngham, and Patrick Mooney had both been seriously wounded. The police had commandeered both the drivers and their vehicles into service. Kepp had suffered a serious gunshot wound to the leg that many believed was caused by an explosive bullet, a projectile that expands on impact, causing horrific wounds.

During the battle another vehicle had accidentally driven into the kill zone. John Carroll, the son of the chief of the Kingstown fire brigade (now Dun Laoghaire), and the driver, Jeremiah Hogan, were both shot dead as they returned from a holiday.[4] One of the men carried a British Military Service card in his pocket, having registered at Birkenhead in January of 1916.[5]

Having assessed all the wounded constables, Dr Hayes decided to send them for further medical attention. Commandant Ashe ordered an immediate medical evacuation of the civilian dead and wounded. The cars that remained serviceable were provided to transport them to the Meath Infirmary in Navan. The wounded constables piled into the cars and the Volunteers watched as the dejected-looking convoy slowly pulled out.

Ashe paraded the remaining R.I.C. prisoners and informed them that if they ever attempted to take up arms against the Republic again they would be shot. He then pardoned them on behalf of the Government of the Irish Republic and permitted them to leave.[6] They made their way slowly into the Ashbourne village where they bought some food and drink.

The Volunteers had suffered one man killed in action and six wounded, one seriously. Joe Taylor, Jack Rafferty, Willie Walsh, Matt Kelly and Ned Rooney were all treated by Dr Hayes. Volunteer Thomas Rafferty was left in a nearby house, as he was too badly wounded to move further. The arms and ammunition that had been taken from the R.I.C. prisoners were loaded into the bread van.

John Austin, one of the men who had witnessed the battle, descended from his vantage point on the hill and made his way onto the road:

> When the firing died down and it was apparent that the battle was over, I went back to the scene. Someone, I can't remember who it was – asked me to take the dead men off the road. I got a horse and cart and proceeded up the road. Tom Ashe and his men were at the crossroads. They were very excited after their victory and were cheering, as men would after a football match. I told Ashe what I was going to do, and he told me to go ahead. Two of the policemen who had not been wounded helped me collect the dead policemen in to the cart. I had eight dead men in the cart when I had finished.[7]

Inspector McCormack, who had been in command of Ashbourne R.I.C. Barracks, asked Austin to convey the bodies to Slane. Austin refused, even after being offered a police escort, stating, 'If we met rebels on the way, what use would your escort be, and where would I be?' Austin placed the bodies in the wash-house at the end of the barracks.

With the huge haul of weapons and ammunition, it was decided to abandon the mission to destroy the railway and return to camp. As each Volunteer section moved out, they were laden down with arms and ammunition. They cycled back to their camp at Borranstown where they had a meal. Weapons were cleaned and checked and extra ammunition was distributed by B.Q.M.S. Lawless.

Later that evening the battalion left Borranstown and made their way to new billets at Newbarn near Kilsallaghan. A small farm was occupied and secured and the men billeted in the outhouses. Outposts were established on the approaches to the camp. Exhausted, many of the men turned in for the night.

Chapter 11

The Beginning of the End

Saturday 29 April 1916 found the Volunteers in good spirits. Morale remained high among the men, even when news reached the camp that Volunteer Thomas Rafferty had died from wounds received during the battle. The son of Dr James Rafferty, Thomas was twenty-two years old and came from Lusk in County Dublin.

Fires were lit and food was in plentiful supply. Those who were not on guard duty spent the morning cleaning their weapons and overhauling and oiling their bicycles. The weapons taken in the previous day's engagement were distributed and each Volunteer held at least three rifles of various designs and a considerable amount of ammunition.

While the officers of the battalion awaited further orders from Dublin many of the men took the chance to wash and clean up. The Volunteers were aware that heavy fighting was taking place in Dublin city because during the day they could hear the sound of artillery and at night the city's burning buildings illuminated the night sky. Having failed to get to Volunteer general headquarters at the General Post Office in Sackville Street, Molly Adrian reported on the situation in Dublin to Commandant Ashe.

Early on Sunday morning 30 April 1916, the Volunteers doubled the guard on the camp as information had been received that a detachment of the 5th Lancers were on their way to attack the encampment. Extra ammunition was distributed and talk among the Volunteers concerned the best ways to repulse an attack by cavalry. There were a number of false alarms during the early hours. Not many slept as each man anticipated an all out attack against their position.

At 11.00 hours on Sunday morning, Sergeant O'Reilly from Swords and Head Constable Keely from Balbriggan, both of the R.I.C., were intercepted on the Kilsallaghan Road. Their vehicle was stopped by sentries and the passengers were ordered to dismount. They requested a meeting with the Volunteers' commanding officer. Ashe was sent for and, along with Lieutenant Mulcahy, Dr Hayes and B.Q.M.S. Frank Lawless, they examined a note produced by the police officers. The note was an order of surrender signed by Patrick Pearse, Commander-in-Chief of the Irish Volunteers.

Ashe was then asked by the police to surrender his force. He refused to believe the R.I.C. officer and considered the note a ruse. He detailed Mulcahy and Lawless to travel to Dublin city to verify the information with Patrick Pearse. The R.I.C. inspector was held as a hostage in order to ensure the safe return of the Volunteers. The authorities issued an official dispatch:

Yesterday (Saturday) the Sinn Féin leaders, including James Connolly, unconditionally surrendered to the General Officer Commanding-in-Chief in Ireland. These leaders, anxious to avoid further bloodshed, have signed a notice to other leaders of their party, both in Dublin and in the country, calling on them to surrender, as their cause is hopeless. These notices are being circulated by the R.I.C. to all stations. A large number of men surrendered last night and this morning, and it is expected that others will follow during the course of the day. A flying column will at once proceed to various points to stimulate the surrender of parties in the country. Emissaries have come from the Sinn Féin party at about Ashbourne, Swords and Wexford to verify the fact of the above surrender with a view to their immediate surrender.[1]

Within an hour and a half the group returned and verified that the note was correct.

The news had a devastating impact on the rank and file and many objected to the idea of surrender. There were groans and catcalls and some of them shouted that it was a trick and that even if the Dublin men had surrendered why should they do so? Mulcahy reminded them that they had come out as soldiers, had behaved as well-disciplined soldiers of Ireland, and that Pearse, whom he had seen, was proud of them. It was his orders that they should now surrender as soldiers. This had a quietening effect on the men and you could feel their pride returning.[2]

While some of the men destroyed their weapons, others sought permission to leave the camp and try to evade capture. Ashe permitted men to leave but others chose to stay and face the consequences.

The officers ordered the men to gather a number of weapons, ammunition, gelignite and detonators. They were placed in wooden boxes, soaked in Rangoon gun oil and three-in-one oil, wrapped in sacking and buried in a trench that had been purposely dug.[3]

As some men left the camp, others sat down, utterly dejected, to await their fate.

With the surrender arranged, the Fingal Volunteers under Commandant Thomas Ashe were marched to Swords. Under armed guard, they were then conveyed in motor lorries to Richmond Barracks in Inchicore, where they were held under guard.

Describing the events in Ashbourne, General Sir John Maxwell, Commander-in-Chief of the British forces in Ireland wrote:

> I received the greatest assistance from the Inspector General, Royal Irish Constabulary, and from all the inspectors and men, and throughout the Rebellion I worked in the closest co-operation with them. In many districts small posts of these gallant men were isolated and had to defend themselves against overwhelming numbers, which they successfully did except in a very few cases.
>
> It was with great regret that I received the report on 28th April that a body of Royal Irish Constabulary, under Inspector Gray, had been ambushed by the rebels at Ashbourne. It was not until the 30th April that I was able to spare a mobile column to deal with this body of rebels, the leaders of which were secured.[4]

Chapter 12

Casualties of War

On Wednesday 10 May 1916, County Inspector Alexander Gray succumbed to his injuries. He was buried on Saturday 13 May with full police honours. The Royal Irish Constabulary band from the Phoenix Park Depot were in attendance and a bugle party from the depot sounded the last post. Inspector Gray was buried alongside his wife, Helen Stewart, in Lucan, in Dublin. There were many floral tributes from the rank and file of the R.I.C. and Captain Shellwell represented the Chief of the British Army in Ireland, General Sir John Grenfell Maxwell.[1]

The Royal Irish Constabulary received a number of awards for their actions during the 1916 Rising. However, the highest award was to Constable Eugene Bratton, Royal Irish Constabulary, who was awarded the King's medal for conspicuous gallantry at Buckingham Palace. He resented having to accept the award.[2]

The actions of the Rising were condemned throughout the country by the media, politicians and the clergy. From the pulpit in Navan, on Sunday 6 May, Father Poland pontificated that 'in this church today rest the mortal remains of eight men who were healthy and stalwart just three days ago and the annals of the happenings of Easter week 1916 will form the darkest records in Irish history.' In a show of solidarity with the police, Bishop Gaughran visited the wounded constables at the infirmary in Navan.[3]

James Quigley, the County Surveyor, whom Volunteer Joe Lawless confronted in the ditch, was implicated in the battle and was accused by the police of relaying information to the Volunteers and leading the police into the trap. He was arrested and charged that 'he did convey information to a number of persons taking part in an armed rebellion and waging war against his Majesty the King.' He was tried by court martial in Richmond Barracks, Inchicore, Dublin. The prosecution stated that Quigley was seen in the vicinity of Rath Cross during the battle and he had been identified by police witnesses as shaking hands with Thomas Ashe.

In his defence Quigley stated that he had been a member of the National Volunteers and when the split had occurred, the Navan corps voted to remain loyal to John Redmond. He denied being in any way involved in the Rising or holding membership of Sinn Féin. He was in the area to give instructions to gangers and supervise men on road-building projects. A number of witnesses spoke in support of Quigley, and when the police involved in the fight in Ashbourne gave evidence against the accused, their case was unconvincing. At the end of the two-day trial, James Quigley was found not guilty of all the charges against him and released.

The unarmed chauffeur Albert Kepp, employed by the Marquis of Conyngham, who had been wounded in the leg during the battle, was removed to hospital. The wound was so severe that he had to have his leg amputated and subsequently died from his injuries. It was widely published that an explosive bullet, a projectile that was outlawed by the articles of war, had caused the injury.

At Richmond Barracks, the Fingal Brigade was held under armed guard with twenty to thirty men in each room. The Volunteers were searched and many had their personal possessions taken. Having taken photographs of the aftermath of the battle, Joe Lawless had his camera confiscated by a British soldier. Some of the Volunteers complained to a British officer and some of the items were returned. However, the camera never materialised.

Word reached the prisoners that when they were questioned by the authorities each man was to state that 'in going out on Easter Monday they were merely obeying as Volunteers the orders of their leaders to mobilise in the ordinary way for manoeuvres.'[4]

Rebels considered suitable for trial are being tried by Field General Court Martial under the defence of the Realm Act in Dublin. As soon as the sentences have been confirmed the public will be informed as to the results of the trial. Those prisoners whose cases could not be immediately dealt with are being sent to places of confinement in England. Their cases will receive consideration later.[5]

On Tuesday morning 2 May 1916, after being questioned by the police and army, many of the prisoners were marched to the North Wall, put in the hold of a cattle boat and transferred to prisons and internment camps in England.

Lieutenant Richard Mulcahy was interned at Knutsford Prison, and later was sent to Frongoch internment camp in Wales until he was released in December 1916.

Some of those who had escaped capture made their way to the United States, while others went on the run only to be picked up later and imprisoned. Volunteer Joseph O'Connor evaded arrest after leaving the Volunteer camp, but was later captured by the Royal Irish Constabulary and escorted to Trinity College by soldiers from the Berkshire Regiment. The following day he was told to go home by the guard commander. He was rearrested by the R.I.C. and held in Santry R.I.C. Barracks. O'Connor was held there for a number of days where he was threatened with execution. He was eventually transferred to Richmond Barracks and then on to England, where he was imprisoned in Wakefield Prison before being sent to Frongoch internment camp in Wales.

On 11 May 1916 Commandant Thomas Ashe was tried by court martial and sentenced to death. Like Eamon De Valera, who was tried at the same time, Ashe's sentence was commuted to life imprisonment. He was transferred to Dartmoor Prison on 23 May 1916.

By December 1916 many Irish Volunteer prisoners were being released under a general amnesty and those who took part in the Battle of Ashbourne returned to Ireland. While imprisoned in England, Ashe was held in Lewes Gaol, then

Portland Prison and finally he was sent to Pentonville, where on 18 June 1917 he was released under the general amnesty. It was while incarcerated in Lewes that Ashe wrote the poem 'Let me carry your Cross for Ireland, Lord'.

On his return to Ireland, Ashe continued the struggle for Irish independence. He spoke at a number of rallies throughout the country, and the authorities issued a warrant for his arrest, charging him with making a seditious speech in Ballinalee, County Longford. Ashe was arrested and held in the Curragh in County Kildare before being transferred to Mountjoy Prison in Dublin. He was convicted and received a two-year sentence with hard labour. Incarcerated in Mountjoy Prison, Ashe and a number of other inmates sought political prisoner status. They requested the right to wear their own clothes and associate with fellow inmates. The authorities refused their request and the prisoners refused to do prison work. In retaliation, the author-ities removed bedding, clothes and personal possessions from the prisoners and their cells. This action caused the protest to escalate and, on 20 September 1917, the prisoners began a hunger strike. Thomas Ashe refused to be branded as a criminal and asserted that, 'Even though I do die, I die in a good cause.'[6]

The authorities began force feeding the prisoners.

On 23 September, Ashe was taken from his cell and escorted to the infirmary, where he was secured to a high wooden chair by leather straps that bound his wrists and ankles. His mouth was prised open with a wooden spoon and a doctor inserted a tube down his neck into the stomach. A mixture of one pint of milk and two eggs was then pumped into the stomach. The procedure lasted between five and ten minutes. The prisoner vomited as the tube was extracted. Ashe was then escorted back to his cell. The procedure was repeated five times on Ashe by Dr Lowe, and on 25 September Ashe collapsed and was transferred to the prison hospital.[7] His condition deteriorated further, and he was removed to the Mater Hospital.

On the night of 25 September 1917, Ashe died. He was thirty-two years old.

The jury returned the following verdict in relation to the inquest on the death of Ashe:

We find that the deceased, Thomas Ashe, according to the medical evidence of Professor M. Weeney, Sir Arthur Chance and Sir Thomas Myles, died from heart failure and congestion of the lungs on the 25th September 1917; that his death was caused by the punishment of taking away from the cell bed, bedding and boots and allowing him to be on the cold floor for up to 50 hours, and then subjecting him to forcible feeding in his weak condition after hunger-striking for five or six days.

We censure the Castle Authorities for not acting more promptly, especially when the grave condition of the deceased and other prisoners were brought under their notice on the previous Saturday by the Lord Mayor and Sir John Irwin.

That the hunger strike was adopted against the inhuman punishment inflicted and a refusal to their demand to be treated as political prisoners.

We condemn forcible and mechanical feeding as an inhuman and dangerous operation, and which should be discontinued.

That the assistant doctor called in, having no previous practice, administered forcible feeding unskilfully.

We find that the taking away of the deceased's bedding and boots was an unfeeling and a barbarous act and we censure the deputy governor for violating the prison rules and inflicting punishment which he had no power to do.

That we infer he was acting under instructions from the Prison Board and Castle, which refused to give evidence and documents asked for.

We tender our sympathy to the relatives of the deceased.[8]

Ashe's remains were first taken to the Pro-Cathedral in Dublin and then transferred to City Hall on Dame Street.

The body of Thomas Ashe lay in state in Dublin's City Hall for two days and tens of thousands passed before it, many weeping, many angry, all sharing a new pride. Through Dublin passed a cortège the like of which had not been seen since the death of Parnell. Leading the marching host were Volunteers in full uniform, carrying rifles. There was a hush over the city at the daring of it. Everyone wondered if the challenge would be accepted, or if the troops would suddenly bar the way of the Volunteers.[9]

As the funeral cortège made its way to Glasnevin cemetery, armed Volunteers drawn from the Fingal Battalion were on duty in case the authorities tried to interfere with the proceedings. A Volunteer guard of honour fired a volley of shots over the coffin as it was lowered into the grave. Michael Collins delivered the graveside oration.

'Nothing additional remains to be said. That volley which we have just heard is the only speech which is proper to make above the grave of a dead Fenian.'[10]

Soon after the death of Thomas Ashe, the Irish War of Independence erupted.

The weapons that had been buried on the day of the surrender of the Fingal Brigade in 1916 were exhumed.[11] Many of those who took part in the Rising once again took up arms in the cause for Irish independence. The type of fighting that took place in Ashbourne would, in time, develop into the guerrilla style tactics that would prove successful for Irish forces during the Irish War of Independence.

Chapter 13

Finale

B.Q.M.S. Frank Lawless was condemned to death for his part in the Rising. However, his sentence was commuted to ten years' penal servitude. He was released from Lewes Gaol in England under a general amnesty in 1917. As a member of Sinn Féin, he was elected to the First Dáil but refused to take a seat in Westminster, London. Elected to the Second Dáil, he was active politically during the Irish War of Independence, and during the Treaty Debates on 7 January 1922 he voted in favour of the ratification of the Treaty. He died in April 1922, aged fifty, after injuries he sustained when the pony and trap he was riding was accidentally upset.

Dr Richard Hayes was sentenced to twenty years' penal servitude for his participation in the Battle of Ashbourne. He was incarcerated in Dartmoor Prison and was later transferred to the Isle of Wight. Before he was released under the general amnesty in 1917, he was transferred to Lewes Gaol. On his return to Ireland, he became politically active within the republican movement and was sentenced to a term in Reading Gaol. During his incarceration, he was elected as M.P. for Limerick. In the Treaty Debates of 1922, he voted in favour of the Treaty. In 1924 he resigned his seat in the Dáil and devoted himself to his medical practice and historical scholarship, writing a number of books. He died peacefully in 1958, aged seventy-six.

On his return to Ireland in late 1916, Lieutenant Richard Mulcahy immediately rejoined the republican movement and was appointed Commandant of the Dublin Brigade of the newly reorganised Irish Republican Army. He, along with Michael Collins, was largely responsible for directing operations during the Irish War of Independence. Mulcahy supported the signing of the Anglo-Irish Treaty and, in the aftermath of Michael Collins' death, was appointed Commander of the newly established Free State Army during the Irish Civil War.

He became notorious during this period for passing an order in relation to captured anti-Treaty forces found in possession of weapons. The order stated that any person found in the possession of arms or ammunition was liable for execution. Under this order the Provisional Government executed seventy-seven anti-Treaty personnel. Richard Mulcahy had a long and distinguished political career and died in 1971 at the age of eighty-five from natural causes.

Captain Richard Coleman, who had been sent to Dublin city at the beginning of the week, fought in the Mendicity Institute. On the general surrender, Coleman was sentenced to death but it was commuted to penal servitude and he was transported to prison in England. On his release under the general amnesty, Captain Coleman continued the struggle for independence. He was soon arrested again, and imprisoned in Mountjoy, taking part in the hunger strike in which Thomas Ashe died. In the months that followed, Coleman found himself transferred from prison to prison in Ireland. After a brief spell out of prison he was rearrested and sent to Usk prison in Wales. Here he contracted pneumonia and died on 7 December 1918. He was twenty-eight years old.

The Civil War that followed the Treaty divided many of those who had stood side by side since 1916. While some refused to take sides, many joined the anti-Treaty forces. Others, like Joe Lawless and Charlie Weston, joined the newly established Free State Army.

Weston achieved the rank of captain and left in 1924, returning to civilian life. Joe Lawless rose to the rank of colonel. His account of the Battle of Ashbourne has been widely published.

On Easter Sunday 26 April 1959, a memorial to the Ashbourne battle was unveiled at the Rath Crossroads in County Meath. The stone structure was designed by Con O'Reilly and Peter Grant, and depicts on one side the figure of Christ and on the other an Irish Volunteer. The inscription reads:

Erected by members of the Fingal Brigade old I.R.A. to commemorate the victorious battle which took place near Ashbourne 28th April 1916 where Volunteers John Crenigan & Thomas Rafferty gave their lives. Designed from the poem 'Let me carry your Cross for Ireland, Lord' composed by their leader Commandant Thomas Ashe.

Let me carry your Cross for Ireland, Lord!
The hour of her trial draws near,
And the pangs and the pain of the sacrifice
May be borne by comrades dear.
But, Lord, take me from the offering throng,
There are many far less prepared,
Though anxious and all as they are to die
That Ireland may be spared.

Let me carry your Cross for Ireland, Lord!
My cares in this world are few,
And few are the tears will fall for me
When I go on my way to you.
Spare, Oh! Spare to the loved ones dear
The brother and son and sire,
That the cause that we love to make may never die
In the land of our heart's desire!

Let me carry your Cross for Ireland, Lord!
Let me suffer the pain and shame:
Bow my head to their rage and hate
And I take on myself the blame.
Let them do with my body whate'er they will,
My spirit I offer to You.
That the faithful few who heard her call
May be spared to Roisin Dhu.

Let me carry your Cross for Ireland, Lord!
For Ireland weak with tears,
For the aged man of the clouded brow
And the child of tender years:

For the empty homes of her golden plains,
For the hopes of her future too,
Let me carry your Cross for Ireland, Lord:
For the cause of Roisin Dhu.[1]

The unveiling was performed by Richard Mulcahy's brother-in-law, President Seán T. O'Kelly. Mulcahy, however, refused to attend the ceremony, and though he did not give a reason, it may have been because he objected to O'Kelly's anti-Treaty stance during the Civil War. In his work *My Father, The General*, Risteárd Mulcahy states that his father had some regrets for the deaths of the policemen; guilt that he believes remained with his father throughout his life.[2]

Chapter 14

The Dumdum

In the weeks and months that followed the Battle of Ashbourne, a number of allegations were made against the Volunteers in relation to the use of 'dumdum' or explosive ammunition. It was stated in the House of Commons that a large quantity of flat-nosed bullets had been found in the ammunition seized from the rebels.[1]

Official reports state that fourteen police officers were wounded in the Battle of Ashbourne. However, other estimates state that there were between thirty and forty constables wounded, and that in the months and years that followed, ten more were to perish from the wounds that they had received during the action.

An expanding or explosive bullet is a projectile designed to expand on impact, increasing in diameter to limit penetration and to produce a larger-scale wound and impart greater stopping power to the target. The typical designs are the hollow-point bullet, the soft-point or soft-nose bullet and the cross-cut. Expanding bullets were given the slang name 'dumdum' after an early British example produced in the Dum Dum Arsenal near Calcutta, India by Captain Neville Bertie Clay. These bullets were developed in response to the growing colonial unrest in the latter part of the nineteenth century. Developed by the British to stop the rush of fanatical tribesmen, many governments protested against the use of such projectiles, arguing that the wounds produced were excessive and inhumane, thus violating the laws of war.

After many years of campaigning, the Hague Convention of 1899, Declaration III, prohibited the use in international warfare of bullets that easily expand or flatten in the body, giving as an example a bullet with jacket with incisions or one that does not fully cover the core.[2] Rather than scrapping the bullets, the British Army continued to use them as practice rounds.

Many historians believe that such rounds were brought in to Ireland by the Irish Volunteers in the shipment of arms and ammunition that were landed from the yacht the *Asgard* at Howth in 1914. In a letter to Joe McGarrity, Patrick Pearse wrote, 'the ammunition landed is useless. It consists of explosive bullets, which are against the rules of civilised warfare, and which we are not serving out to the men.'[3]

During the House of Commons debates on the subject, it was stated that 'there was no official information as to the source from which these bullets were obtained by the rebels.'[4]

It is of course possible that such ammunition could have been imported into the country, but other possibilities regarding the wounds that the police officers received must be examined.

One possibility is that the Mauser ammunition was mistaken for explosive rounds.

The Mauser rifle was one of the earliest bolt-action military rifles. The cartridge discharged was an eleven-millimetre utilising a .446 diameter bullet weighing three hundred and seventy grains. The military load for this weapon had a three hundred and eighty-six grain bullet launched at one thousand four hundred and twenty-five feet per second. When fired in close engagements it often resulted in similar wounds to that of an explosive bullet.

In some of the witness statements in relation to Ashbourne, the Volunteers state that they seized what they believed was explosive ammunition from the police stations that they had raided that week. It is possible that the police, like the British Army, were using explosive rounds as practice rounds.

There is no doubt that the wounds inflicted during the battle were of a serious nature and resembled those that may occur when an explosive bullet is used.

During the Battle of Ashbourne, the Irish Volunteers made use of American Winchester shotguns. The use of shotguns at close range has been known to produce horrific wounds. At fifteen feet the ammunition spray from a shotgun forms a tight pattern. As the distance increases, the pellets spread out, roughly one inch to every one yard travelled. The shotgun is most effective within fifty yards of a target. During World War One, the German government denounced the use of pump-action shotguns and unsuccessfully petitioned the international courts in an attempt to outlaw their use in warfare, stating that the weapon was barbaric.

The Battle of Ashbourne took place at very close range. The hydraulic pressures built up by very high velocity close-range projectiles inflict permanent cavitations and cause traumatic wounds. This can be said of bullets used by all nationalities.

Many bullets of the period followed a similar design and consisted of a heavy core, generally lead that was surrounded by a jacket of copper, nickel or steel.

In 1914, writing from the Western Front, Captain Noel Chavasse of the Royal Army Medical Corp stated that:

> The wounds one had to dress were not the clean punctures I had imagined gunshot wounds to be, but because of the near range that at first made one to think they had been made by explosive bullets… to take an instance of a wound in a fleshly part of the thigh, the entrance wound was neat and punctured, but the exit was a gaping burst, a big hole that I could put my fist into, with broken muscles hanging out. As a matter of fact, I believe that at such near range, the bullet turns over and over, and practically bursts it way out.[5]

The propaganda machine of the British administration in Ireland seized on the opportunity to vilify the rank and file of the Volunteer movement. While it is possible that some of these rounds were fired, it is doubtful that large amounts of this type of round were brought into the country during the Howth gun running. The use of explosive bullets during the 1916 Rising is still open to question and further research on the topic is required.

Today, the use of expanding bullets is legal, as the Hague Convention only applies to the use of such bullets during war. Expanding rounds are often used in hunting or law enforcement where a target needs to be neutralised quickly in order to prevent further danger or loss of life.

Chapter 15

Turning the Tide of Battle

The Royal Irish Constabulary tried to excuse their defeat at Ashbourne by stating that their force had been ambushed. An ambush is defined as an attack from a concealed position, but on examination of the engagement at Ashbourne, it is clear that the Irish Volunteers were taken as much by surprise as the arriving members of the Royal Irish Constabulary. The Battle of Ashbourne was not an ambush, but a bold flanking movement that helped to restore momentum during an attack, enabling the Volunteers to defeat a numerically superior force.

Outflanking is the turning of a flank, an attack on the rear or the total encirclement of a force. It offers the opportunity to neutralise the strongest part of an enemy force, namely its centre or front. By appearing from an unexpected direction or simply overlapping the enemy's flanks to cause panic, an attacking army can also inflict a psychological blow on an enemy. If an enemy is simultaneously engaged from the front, flanking also offers the chance to bring more fire to bear.[1]

The rapid reaction by the Volunteers to the developing situation enabled them to gain the upper hand. Two unexpected factors made it costly to the police: the area's convoluted topography and the resourcefulness of the attacking Volunteers in converting that terrain to their tactical advantage. Thanks in part to Mulcahy's tenacity and quick thinking, it was realised that the position of the police was precarious, and that they could be outflanked and attacked from a number of directions.

Initially, the Royal Irish Constabulary had the element of surprise. A large force, outnumbering the Volunteers, arrived on the scene as the Volunteers were attacking the barracks. The police stopped their vehicles on the high ground, thus gaining an immediate advantage over the Volunteers. If the police had pressed home the attack and deployed to the fields from the road they would have outflanked the Volunteers before they had the chance to deploy their forces in an aggressive counter-attack. The weight of numbers would have forced the Volunteers to retreat or surrender. The easiest way to avoid being flanked is to retreat before you are completely cut off. Maintaining a high level of operational awareness on the battlefield through reconnaissance and communication is essential for every commander.

On examination of the police tactics, one may see that the Royal Irish Constabulary seriously underestimated their enemy. Inspector Gray's force was overconfident, having a long record of defeating insurgents throughout the country. This quasi-military force was well armed and well trained. Gray's idea of using a mobile 'flying squad' to track and capture the Volunteers was a good idea, but his lack of intelligence regarding the size of the insurgent force, their capabilities and their exact location contributed to his defeat. When the Volunteers questioned the captured police officers it materialised that they had received orders not to take any prisoners.[2] The defeat of the police at Ashbourne showed the Irish people that the Constabulary were not as invincible as they thought – a point that would be remembered in the years that were to follow.

Unfair criticism is often levelled against Thomas Ashe for his actions during the battle. Though Richard Mulcahy is credited with turning the tide of battle, it was the combination of Mulcahy's and Ashe's leadership and the quality of the men under their command that resulted in the victory. Acting on battlefield reports, Ashe prepared to withdraw his men when faced with what he believed was a superior force, but on listening to Mulcahy's plan, he belayed that order.

He agreed to Mulcahy's flanking manoeuvre, implementing an aggressive attack that resulted in the defeat and capture of a large force of Constabulary. If a difference of opinion had developed between the officers during the battle, the Irish Volunteers would have faced certain defeat and capture. Both of these men worked closely together and relayed clearly the information to their respective commands. Both officers remained with their men during the battle, moving from post to post. Ashe's battlefield management is often called into question by historians, yet his action as commandant during the battle, listening to his subordinate, taking the advice to hand and ordering the flanking manoeuvre goes some way to proving that Ashe was a capable officer. The leadership of the 5th Battalion of the Irish Volunteers had transformed the unit from a small, semi-independent group of raiders into a significant military force.

During the Battle of Ashbourne, the close-quarter fighting and the terrain contributed greatly to the confusion of both sides. Towards the end of the battle, the Volunteers found themselves in a friendly-fire incident. Now known by soldiers as a 'Blue on Blue', friendly fire or fratricide is the inadvertent firing towards one's own or otherwise friendly force while attempting to engage the enemy. The primary cause of such incidents may be described as the 'fog of war', which attributes friendly fire incidents to the confusion inherent in warfare. Such incidents are exacerbated by the close proximity of combatants.

Questions arise in relation to the number of participants that were involved from both sides. Official reports state that Inspector Gray had sixty-four men in Slane. He travelled to Ashbourne with fifty-four police officers in seventeen motorcars, leaving a small rearguard in Slane.[3] The police barracks in Ashbourne had been reinforced the day before the battle and the force there numbered fifteen. This brought the total number of police involved to sixty-nine. It is possible that a number of civilian drivers were mistakenly counted as combatants and included in the final count of participants.

The rank and file of the Volunteers were a disciplined force and well trained, and this is reflected in their deployment during the battle. The mobility of the Volunteers gave the impression that there were more in action than were actually there. The Volunteers attacked the barracks with three sections that consisted of thirty-six men and their two senior officers, Ashe and Mulcahy. Towards the end of the battle, B.Q.M.S. Frank Lawless arrived with another six Volunteers. This brought the total number to forty-five. A small force was left behind to guard the camp.

In the aftermath of the battle, both sides exaggerated the numbers that had been involved, one side exaggerating their victory, the other side as an excuse for their defeat.

In relation to the police surrender, official reports state that they fought until they had expended their last cartridge, and when they saw that further resistance was useless they surrendered.[4] A debate arose in the House of Commons asking why the police were compelled, owing to the lack of ammunition, to surrender at discretion with the loss of so many men. It was stated that:

Two officers and fifty-four men of the Royal Irish Constabulary took part in the Ashbourne affray on 28th April. The fighting lasted for five hours, when both officers had fallen and six of the men had been killed and fifteen wounded, the remainder surrendered, being completely surrounded by about 300 rebels and having practically at that time exhausted their ammunition.[5]

This statement is suspicious as, after the battle, the Volunteers recalled in their witness statements that they collected hundreds of rounds of ammunition from their prisoners.

Manoeuvrability was vital during the battle, and the Irish Volunteers achieved this by fighting in small, compact sections. The guerrilla tactics that were developed by the Irish Republican Army following the Battle of Ashbourne were to influence insurgent forces throughout the world. These same tactics were to be written down and passed from group to group, a textbook guide to defeating a numerically superior force.

In rough terrain, retreat and disappear until the enemy is strung out in pursuit. Then concentrate on one weak point. Time, space and retreat are the instruments of combat victors. When fighting an enemy who has superior numbers and equipment, success lies in mobility...

In a sustained guerrilla action, the groups of guerrillas can only be successful if they have a rigid and completely centralised command. The central command post directing guerrillas in operation should never be further from the actual fighting than a man can trot in half an hour.[6]

The strategy and tactics of guerrilla warfare tend to focus around the use of small, mobile forces against a larger, superior one. Organising in small units, they often depend on the support of the local population. They take advantage of terrain and seek to avoid confrontation with large numbers of enemy troops. They prefer to engage small groups of soldiers to minimise loss and gradually exhaust the opposing force. Constant attacks on enemy personnel and resources seek to weaken the enemy so that they are unable to wage war and are forced to capitulate.

During the Irish War of Independence, the same tactics employed by the Volunteers at Ashbourne were repeated. On 19 March 1921, British troops acting on intelligence converged on the area of Crossbarry in County Cork in an operation to destroy the West Cork Brigade of the Irish Republican Army under the command of Commandant Tom Barry. Moving rapidly in a series of motorised convoys, Crown forces had made their way to four points, about four miles north, north-east, south-south-east and west of Crossbarry. A mobile convoy consisting of over one thousand British troops supported by

Auxiliaries converged on the area. Commandant Barry realised that he had to engage the enemy because any attempt to withdraw his force may result in their destruction or capture. Possessing detailed knowledge of the local terrain, he ordered his flying column to mobilise and make ready to attack the advancing British troops. Barry divided his small force into seven sections and moved rapidly into a number of positions.

The British had divided their force into two columns with the object of surrounding the Irish Brigade. Under the command of Major Percival, the British attacked from the east and south, from where they were repulsed. Another British attack was made from the west and was again repulsed. At the left rear of the position, two hundred British troops made an attempt to break through the Irish line. Volunteers were rushed to this area to reinforce the position. Volley fire was opened up on the advancing British troops, forcing them to retire with heavy losses.

Having regrouped, British troops renewed their attack and attempted once again to encircle the Irish position. Any attempt by British troops to break through the Irish lines was thwarted. The British formation broke, and they withdrew having suffered heavy casualties.

In the engagement at Crossbarry, Irish forces suffered three Volunteers killed and two wounded. British Crown forces listed thirty-nine killed, including five officers, and forty-seven wounded. Using similar tactics to those that were employed at Ashbourne in 1916, the Irish Republican Army had managed to defeat a numerically superior enemy force and then successfully withdraw from the field of battle.[7]

The Battle of Ashbourne had considerable significance for small mobile forces throughout the world. Strategically it was important because it provided an example of how a detailed knowledge of local terrain could be used to great advantage against an enemy. Tactically, however, the battle was even more significant. It defined the means by which the future war in Ireland would be fought and won, county-by-county.

Epilogue

It may surprise the reader that, with the exception of Inspector Harry Smyth, all those who fought during the Battle of Ashbourne 1916 were Irish. These men, both Royal Irish Constabulary and Irish Volunteers, had lived and worked in the same areas and in many cases they were known to each other. Families would have often interacted through church, schools and local businesses. Local police stations and their officers would have played an important part in the community.

However, behind this façade of normal, everyday life in Ireland, British imperial policy had divided the nation's population and a legacy of mistrust and hatred had, over time, spread amongst the people. The Land Wars of the late nine-teenth century had marginalised the police in Ireland, an action from which the force would never recover.

Severity breedeth fear, but roughness breedeth hatred.[1]

The force was marginalised even further when, in 1919, the Royal Irish Constabulary found itself in a guerrilla war against the Irish Republican Army. Unable to cope with the increased attacks on the R.I.C., the British Government recruited thousands of ex-soldiers to supplement the force in units such as the Black and Tans and the Auxiliaries. Many of these men were Irish, and their reign of terror in the form of reprisals and extrajudicial killings have left an indelible bloody mark in Irish history.

While many people believe that the opening shots of the Irish Civil War were fired in 1922, a deep division had, for centuries, been growing among the Irish population. Some historians and political scientists define a civil war (as opposed to a civil disturbance) as involving a minimum of one thousand casualties. In Ireland, the death toll far exceeded that. The horror and brutality of the Irish War of Independence is closely linked to the fact that Irishmen were fighting each other, a fact that was to be repeated from 1922 to 1923.

War in general may be a brutal affair, but civil war generates viciousness amongst friends, families and neighbours that may never dissipate. A divided country may be united by moving a land boundary. A divided population is a cause for great concern, as even after a civil war, tensions will remain for generations to come.

Endnotes

Foreword
1 Rees, R., *Ireland 1905-25; Vol 1. Text and Historiography* (Colour Print Books, Newtownards, 1998)
2 Connolly, S.J., *The Oxford Companion to Irish History* (Oxford University Press, 2002)

Chapter 1
1 MacNeill, E., *Sunday Independent*, Dublin edition, 23 April 1916
2 Lawless, J., Witness Statement 1043 (Bureau of Military History 1913-1921, Dublin)
3 Weston, C., Witness Statement 149 (Bureau of Military History 1913-1921, Dublin)
4 Hayes, R., Witness Statement 97 (Bureau of Military History 1913-1921, Dublin)
5 Lawless, J., Witness Statement 1043 (Bureau of Military History 1913-1921, Dublin)

Chapter 2
1 Lawless J., Witness Statement 1043 (Bureau of Military History 1913-1921, Dublin)

2 Hayes, R., Witness Statement 97 (Bureau of Military History 1913-1921, Dublin)

3 Hayes, R., Witness Statement 97 (Bureau of Military History 1913-1921, Dublin)

4 McAllister, M., Witness Statement 1494 (Bureau of Military History 1913-1921, Dublin)

5 W/O 903/19 PT2

6 Weston, C., Witness Statement 149 (Bureau of Military History 1913-1921, Dublin)

7 Lawless, J., Witness Statement 1043 (Bureau of Military History 1913-1921, Dublin)

Chapter 3

1 W/O 903/19 PT2

2 O'Brien, P., *Crossfire: The Battle of the Four Courts, 1916* (New Island, Dublin, 2012)

3 Lawless, J., Witness Statement 1043 (Bureau of Military History 1913-1921, Dublin)

4 Golden, J., Witness Statement 521 (Bureau of Military History 1913-1921, Dublin)

5 A Volunteer Officer, *The Battle of Ashbourne* (The National Library of Ireland, 1942, IR. 941091 H7)

Chapter 4

1 Lawless, J., Witness Statement 1043 (Bureau of Military History 1913-1921, Dublin)

2 Kelly, James, *Midland Tribune*, 1916 Jubilee Supplement

3 McAllister, M., Witness Statement 1494 (Bureau of Military History 1913-1921, Dublin)

4 Lawless, J., Witness Statement 1043 (Bureau of Military History 1913-1921, Dublin)

5 Golden, J. Witness Statement 521 (Bureau of Military History 1913-1921, Dublin)

Chapter 5

1 Weston, C., Witness Statement 149 (Bureau of Military History 1913-1921, Dublin)
2 Weston, C., Witness Statement 149 (Bureau of Military History 1913-1921, Dublin)
3 CO 903/19
4 Ashbourne, 28 April 1916', *Riocht na Midhe*, 2003, Vol. 14, pp 194-229

Chapter 6

1 Austin, J., Witness Statement 904 (Bureau of Military History 1913-1921, Dublin)
2 *The Constabulary Gazette*, April-August 1916
3 Golden, J., Witness Statement 521 (Bureau of Military History 1913-1921, Dublin)

Chapter 7

1 Bratton, E., Witness Statement 467 (Bureau of Military History 1913-1921, Dublin)
2 Weston, C., Witness Statement 149 (Bureau of Military History 1913-1921, Dublin)
3 *The Constabulary Gazette*, April-August 1916
4 Lawless, J.V., 'The Battle of Ashbourne' in Diarmuid Ferriter (ed.), *Dublin's Fighting Story* (Mercier Press, Cork, 2010, pp 117-30)
5 McAllister, M., Witness Statement 1494 (Bureau of Military History 1913-1921, Dublin)

Chapter 9

1 Weston, C., Witness Statement 149 (Bureau of Military History 1913-1921, Dublin)
2 *The Constabulary Gazette*, April-August 1916

Chapter 10

1 A Volunteer Officer, *The Battle of Ashbourne* (The National Library of Ireland, 1942, IR. 941091 H7)
2 Mulcahy, R., Richard Hayes Leabhar Cuimhneacháin (Cumann Cabhartha Sean Óglach Fhine Gall, 1916)
3 O'Connor, J., Witness Statement 142 (Bureau of Military History 1913-1921, Dublin)
4 WO 35/69
5 *The Constabulary Gazette*, April-August 1916
6 O'Connor, J., Witness Statement 142 (Bureau of Military History 1913-1921, Dublin)
7 Austin, J., Witness Statement 904 (Bureau of Military History 1913-1921, Dublin)

Chapter 11

1 Maxwell, J.G., Official Statement from Irish Command April 1916 WO 35/69
2 McAllister, M., Witness Statement 1494 (Bureau of Military History 1913-1921, Dublin)
3 Golden J., Witness Statement 521 (Bureau of Military History 1913-1921, Dublin)
4 Maxwell, J.G., Official Statement from Irish Command, May 1916 WO 35/69

Chapter 12

1 *The Constabulary Gazette*, April-August 1916
2 Bratton, E., Witness Statement 467 (Bureau of Military History 1913-1921, Dublin)
3 Coogan, O., *Politics and War in Meath 1913-23* (Folens & Co., Dublin, 1983)
4 Hayes, R., Witness Statement 876 (Bureau of Military History 1913-1921, Dublin)

5 Maxwell, J.G, Official Statement from Irish Command Headquarters, May 1916

6 O'Luing, S., *I Die in a Good Cause* (Anvil, Kerry, 1970)

7 Golden, J., Witness Statement 522 (Bureau of Military History 1913-1921, Dublin)

8 O'Luing, S., *I Die in a Good Cause* (Anvil, Kerry, 1970)

9 Gallagher, F., *Four Glorious Years 1918-1921* (Irish Press, Dublin, 1953)

10 Collins, M. Graveside Oration at the funeral of Thomas Ashe, 1917

11 Golden, J., Witness Statement 522 (Bureau of Military History 1913-1921, Dublin)

Chapter 13

1 O'Luing, S., *I Die in a Good Cause* (Anvil, Kerry, 1970)

2 Mulcahy, R., *My Father, The General* (Liberties Press, Dublin, 2011)

Chapter 14

1 HC Deb, 22 May 1916

2 Hague Convention Declaration III 1899

3 Cronin, S., *The McGaritty Papers* (Anvil, Kerry, 1972)

4 HC Deb, 31 May 1916

5 Chavasse, N., Private Letter, Imperial War Museum, 1914

Chapter 15

1 Johnson, R., *How to Win on the Battlefield* (Thames & Hudson Ltd, London, 2010)

2 Hayes, R., Witness Statement 97 (Bureau of Military History 1913-1921, Dublin)

3 CO 904/120

4 *Daily Mail*, 2 May 1916

5 HC Deb, June 1916
6 Tse-Tung, Mao, *Guerrilla Warfare* (China, 1937)
7 Barry, T., *Guerrilla Days in Ireland* (Anvil, Dublin, 1962)

Epilogue
1 Bacon, F., *Of Innovations: Essays* (Penguin, London, 1985)

Select Bibliography

Barry, T., *Guerrilla Days in Ireland* (Anvil, Dublin, 1962)

Bateson, R., *They Died by Pearse's Side* (Irish Graves Publications, Dublin, 2010)

Caulfield, M., *The Easter Rebellion* (Gill & Macmillan, Dublin, 1995)

Coogan, O., *Politics and War in Meath 1913-23* (Folens & Co., Dublin, 1983)

Johnson, R., *How to Win on the Battlefield* (Thames & Hudson Ltd, London, 2010)

Kelleher, T., *Rebel Cork's Fighting Story 1916-1921* (Mercier Press, Cork, 2009)

Lawless, J.V., 'The Battle of Ashbourne' in Diarmuid Ferriter (ed.), *Dublin's Fighting Story* (Mercier Press, Cork, 2010, pp 117-30)

Mao, Tse-tung, *Guerrilla Warfare* (China, 1937)

Mulcahy, R., My Father, The General (Liberties Press, Dublin, 2011)

O'Luing, S., *I Die in a Good Cause* (Anvil, Kerry, 1970)

O'Brien, P., *Crossfire: The Battle of the Four Courts, 1916* (New Island, Dublin, 2012)

O'Reilly, T., *Our Struggle for Independence* (Mercier Press, Cork, 2009)

Rees, R., *Ireland 1905-25: Vol 1. Text and Historiography* (Colour Print Books, Newtownards, 1998)

Von Clausewitz, Carl, *On War* (ed. & trans. Michael Howard & Peter Paret, Princeton University Press, Princeton, 1832/1976)

Index

1916 IN FOCUS

Crossfire
The Battle of the Four
Courts, 1916

Paul O'Brien

On Easter Monday 1916, Commandant Edward Daly, commanding the 1st Battalion of the Irish Volunteers, occupied the Four Courts and the surrounding area.

Ensconced in a labyrinth of streets, alleyways and tenement buildings, Daly and the Volunteers created a killing ground that would witness some of the fiercest fighting of the 1916 Rising.

Surrounded and outgunned, the Volunteers held their positions and were the last Battalion of the Rising to surrender.

Confronted by such a determined foe, British military forces were forced to rethink their strategy in order to regain control of the second city of the Empire.

Crossfire is the true story of one of the bloodiest engagements against Crown forces during the 1916 Rising. It examines the battles that were fought in and around the Four Courts area of Dublin city, and the atrocities that were uncovered on North King Street as the rising came to an end.

ISBN 978-1-84840-129-7
Spring 2012

Shootout
The Battle of St Stephen's Green, 1916

Paul O'Brien

As the Proclamation of the Irish Republic was being read from the steps of the General Post Office on Sackville Street on Easter Monday 24th April 1916, one hundred and sixty members of the Irish Citizen Army under Commandant Michael Mallin were taking up position within Dublin city.

For seven days, from their posts in St Stephen's Green and City Hall, this small force of men and women would fight against British soldiers as they struggled to protect this newly proclaimed Irish Republic.

City fights involve harsh battlegrounds that place extraordinary demands on the combatants, and the battleground for Dublin city was no exception. For almost a century,

Commandant Michael Mallin and his force have been criticised by some for their actions during that Easter week. Accusations of being strategically deficient and unorganised have been levelled against Commandant Mallin, yet this commander, outnumbered and outgunned, carried out his orders and fought with great tenacity.

Although many stories about the Rising are well known, and have been retold in books and documentaries that have transformed Easter 1916 into something of a national myth synonymous with courage and fortitude, some of these stories remain untold until now.

Shootout is a detailed account of the military actions of Commandant Michael Mallin and his command.

ISBN 978-1-84840-211-9
Spring 2013